Successful Digital Marketing
In a Week

Nick Smith

D0591461

The Teach Yourself series has been trusted around the world
for over sixty years. This series of 'In A Week' business books
is designed to help people at all levels and around the world to
further their careers. Learn in a week, what the experts learn in
a lifetime.

Nick Smith runs a successful online marketing consultancy advising companies how to increase sales and profits using the power of the internet and by leveraging forgotten assets hidden in their business. Companies hire Nick and his team to devise effective traffic strategies using a combination of paid marketing sources, search engine optimization and social media marketing. In addition, Nick is considered to be one of the leading direct response marketing consultants in the UK after logging more than 33,000 hours implementing successful online marketing strategies during the past 12 years. In his spare time, Nick writes for his blog (NickTheGeek.com) and also maintains CamStudio (CamStudio.org), the world's most popular free desktop recording software downloaded 100,000 times every week.

Teach® Yourself

Successful Digital Marketing

Nick Smith

www.inaweek.co.uk

IN A WEEK

Contents

Introduction

Hello my fellow Marketing Warriors ...

What, that isn't what you want to be?

Sorry, but whether or not you like it very much it is war out there.

That makes you a warrior and that means you need this book.

This book is what I consider essential basic training for every small business owner or department manager before they hope to trek deeper into the marketing woods.

This book that you are about to read is broader than my other books *Teach Yourself Successful Social Media Marketing in a Week* and *Teach Yourself Successful SEO and Search Marketing In A Week*. I'm giving you the broad strokes to train you in the basics of what you need to know to survive and thrive with marketing in this digital age.

It's not our parents' world anymore, where direct mail, TV commercials, and billboards ruled. Now we have to adapt to changes and change fast ourselves, especially in the area of mobile marketing (discussed later in the week).

More than just this, of course, this book gives you the low-down on all the topics you will need:

● Social marketing
● Search engine optimization
● 'Paid' advertising on Google/Facebook, and so on
● Creating the perfect website that makes sales
● And more ... (Lots of tips and tricks on everything from Yahoo Answers to press releases)

A word for those whom this book isn't for:
The goal of these tips is that you don't get seduced by the siren call of all the gimmicks out there. There is always another 'push button traffic' tool or 'magic bullet' product that will try to get your attention (and money).

If you are looking for a 'get-rich-quick' book, this is not it. Everything, including your website, requires planning and work – work that doesn't always deliver return on investment overnight.

If you stick at it and follow the principles laid down in this book, then you will get the results you want sure enough.

If you are reading this part in the sample reading section of Amazon:

Why haven't you bought the book yet?

You have to pay to play and buying this book is an investment in your education if ever there was one.

Don't worry I'll wait ...

All right, enough metaphors and feel good stuff. Let's get cracking and, first of all, let's deal with the most pivotal point of the whole equation, your website because that's almost certainly where you will be sending all your traffic to.

Does it make the grade? Let's find out ...

SUNDAY

Building the ultimate sales website

Welcome to the starting line of your 'digital marketing' race.

This is more of a marathon then a sprint but as the saying goes 'The journey of a thousand miles begins with one step'.

So take what you learn in this book and *apply it* as this can change you and your business for the better.

And so to begin, before we get into the 'sexy' stuff, like social media marketing and search engine optimization, we need to talk about some far more important things.

First, we need to talk about your website, because all the traffic in the world will not make you money if you have a crappy website that can't convert all those visitors into buyers.

This is where you really start to make money.

At the same time you don't want to spend too much time trying to fine-tune every detail on the site but not enough time on generating traffic.

The key here is to practice a little 'Kaizen'– the art of continuous improvement.

Just get started with a decent (though not perfect) website and make small improvements when you need to as your traffic grows and builds over the long haul.

SUNDAY

MONDAY

TUESDAY

WEDNESDAY

THURSDAY

FRIDAY

SATURDAY

Look and feel

So first off you need to find your perfect 'look and feel'– what should this be?

Check out your competition to see what kind of 'look' their websites have. Take notes of what you like and what you don't.

Take a look at company websites in different sectors. Is there anything you like on those sites that your competition *aren't* utilizing?

Now ask yourself a question ... Who are you? What makes you unique in this world? What's your personality? Sarcastic? Funny? Thoughtful?

The perfect look and feel for you and your business is a combination of all these things.

It should be a reflection of what makes you unique in this world. If you're an accountant with a great sense of humour, inject a little of that into your website. Accountants don't have to all be boring (kidding).

For a perfect example of this, take Sir Richard Branson. His various Virgin websites are still very corporate looking but have enough of his personality in them to make them stand out.

Why can't you do the same?

Organization

Next your website needs to be easy to move around. Your visitors want to quickly find what they're looking for. Once they come to your site and you're able to answer their questions and show them what they need, they may want the answers to other questions as well.

So make it as easy as possible for them. Interlink within your posts to other posts at the beginning, at various places in the middle and also at the end.

Essentially be plugging your other content as much as possible without going overboard.

Lay out your navigation bar logically and make sure that your most popular pages are highlighted.

This will get people clicking around your site, which looks good to Google, which looks great to your bottom line.

If you need help with this, again check your competition and other websites not in your sector for ideas.

Landing pages and sales pages

First some definitions.

A landing page is where your visitor enters your site and a sales page is where you offer to sell them something and they make the choice to buy or not.

The two aren't necessarily the same thing, although they can be.

It depends on what you're promoting, and whether your potential visitors are likely to be offended with a gentle sales message as soon as they get to your website and so on.

The 'sales funnel'

The idea with the sales funnel is to guide your visitors through your site to eventually land on a related sales page where you can try to persuade them to buy your product or service. The question you need to ask is 'What does my visitor really want?'

How do you get them to do this? This is the main question you need to answer and the main way to answer this question is to think about what the visitor wants.

If they've just done a search on Google for 'dog grooming service Hoboken', they probably don't need educating as to the benefits of professional dog grooming, they're ready to hire, so take them to a page with a little sales copy explaining why they should hire 'you' and a 'buy' button or your phone number so they can get in touch.

If they searched for 'dog grooming techniques', then the landing page could be a nice article explaining some basic techniques that owners could use and then maybe offer a free video showing you doing the techniques in exchange for their email address (building a prospect list) enabling you to follow up with them via email, increasing your chances of getting a client or making a sale.

(I talk about email marketing on Friday.)

Money making ninja tip

If you can also capture the visitor's state/province/county at the same time as capturing their email address, you could earn additional revenue by taking those leads you would normally ignore and selling them on to non-competing 'dog grooming' businesses in different locations.

Speak to your techie about this – it's really easy to do and could be very profitable.

Anyway, you get the picture.

The only exception to this would be if you are an online company, perhaps a software company, and all you do is sell your software and have other people educate for you and send them to your sales website.

But, in that case you are probably not reading this book anyway!

So as you can see there are essentially two main sales funnels, direct and indirect, via email. I recommend having both for your business.

A third model – the webinar

There is a third model that is a mix between email and sales and that is the webinar model.

A webinar is just like a presentation that you do online (you talking into a webcam and/or a slide-based presentation) and that can be watched and listened to by hundreds of people at once.

This works particularly well if you offer a high-ticket product or service. You promote a special event giving away some excellent information for free that solves a big problem for your visitors and then, at the end of the webinar, you make attendees aware of your product or service (with a corresponding high price tag) for those that are interested, with no pressure.

You can add the names of those that sign up to attend the webinar to a mailing list so the other email marketing rules still apply and, while the sales volume may be lower, the actual money made can be higher, depending on the business.

In the dog groomers example, this could be a week's vacation for their pooch including grooming, pampering, special training and so on.

If you sell a physical item, maybe bundle it up with other items or partner with someone who can offer a related service and split the profits.

Any businesses can offer a 'premium' version of their product or service. It just requires a little thought.

Once you know what you're selling, what next?

Tracking

Now is the time to start tracking your visitors on your website. Where do they spend the most time?

How many pages do they view?

Where do they land the most frequently and from there where do they click?

Are your visitors mostly mobile?

And of course the most important question:

What percentage of visitors buy?

All these and more are questions that you must answer to have the ultimate sales website.

Only in this way can you see what is really working and what isn't. You may be getting a lot of traffic to one page but the visitors end up leaving quickly or not going to another page. Why? Who knows but you need to find out. Go and check out that page, and see whether you can spice it up.

Actually, you can do all this by having analytics software installed on your website.

This is very easy to do – literally copying and pasting a code into every page you want to track or into your website's design template (if you have software like WordPress or Magneto eCommerce).

I recommend using either Google Analytics (GA) or Clicky.

GA is free and can directly interface between your Google AdWords and Google Webmaster Tools accounts to get the maximum amount of data possible.

Clicky is perfect if you're worried about information overload because the interface is a lot simpler.

Spend time getting to know the interface and go through the settings one by one. There are lots of settings and I could write a full book on them alone.

Google provides a couple of excellent free resources where you can learn everything you need to know to get up to speed with GA:

www.youtube.com/googleanalytics?hl=en
www.google.com/analytics/learn

You can sign up for Clicky here: http://clicky.com

There are lots of tutorials on YouTube for both Clicky and GA – just do a search for 'Clicky analytics' or 'Google Analytics.'

If you use WordPress to power your website, you can integrate both their GA and Clicky in just a couple of mouse clicks by installing related plug-ins.

Use analytics to track the changes that had a positive increase on your pages, then replicate them on others and see what happens.

Split testing

Once you have traffic and are tracking where your visitors come from, where they go on your website and what kind of conversion rates you get, it's time to start split testing your sales and order pages.

One simple way is to use Content Experiments by Google Analytics. It's pretty easy to set up and once you have done so, each of your visitors will be shown one or other of the pages in the Experiment automatically. When set up correctly, you'll be able to track right the way through to a sale or whatever the action is that you want to track.

(Again there are videos on YouTube showing you how to do this, or hire a geek on a freelancer site like oDesk.com, eLance.com to do it for you.)

When you do this, don't send them to two entirely different pages. Only make a small change to the second page, that is, change the 'buy now' button to an 'add to cart' button or change the button colour. Small changes like this can make a huge difference.

Change the font to something easier to read. Change the headline at the top of the page. And on and on.

Keep in mind that you should *only change one thing at a time*. If you change multiple things at the same time, there is really no way to know why the page is doing better or worse than the other page.

There's a great free Content Experiments tutorials video here courtesy of Google Developers:

http://lk.gs/2

In conclusion

The key is to start getting your website out there. A perfect site doesn't exist. But imperfect sites make money every single day if they get traffic.

So make a site that matches your personality and get going.

I was once involved in a project back in my beginner days with a doctor who wanted the 'perfect' website. He paid upwards of $20,000 for everything he wanted custom made. Problem is when he opened up the site he found out nobody really wanted what he offered. He eventually ran out of money and had to go back to work as a doctor.

Don't be that person.

Summary

If you go through the things recommended in this chapter today, you should have a website capable of making sales within a short period of time.

But don't just rest on your laurels. Keep tweaking, testing, tweaking and testing until it becomes second nature.

If there is one constant in marketing, it is that you and your market will always be changing!

Things that worked a year ago don't work now. Those that work now might not work as well a year from now.

So keep an eye on your website (or hire someone once it is making money to do that for you) and it will be a source of income for years to come.

So now we have the first set of questions to make sure that you've taken everything on board ...

SUNDAY

MONDAY

TUESDAY

WEDNESDAY

THURSDAY

FRIDAY

SATURDAY

Questions

1. When building your site, you need to have:
   a) The ultimate sales website right out of the gate ❏
   b) A good site to start and the ultimate site later ❏
   c) A bad site to start and the ultimate later ❏

2. Landing pages are:
   a) Pages that are fallen on sometimes, causing them to break ❏
   b) The first page your visitor sees ❏
   c) The place you sell your visitor stuff ❏

3. Sales pages are:
   a) Pages that people should come to first ❏
   b) Pages that people should come to second ❏
   c) Pages that people should come to when ready ❏
   d) Pages that are basically the same as landing pages ❏

4. How many sales funnels are out there?
   a) 1 ❏
   b) 2 ❏
   c) 3 ❏
   d) 4 ❏

5. These sales funnels include:
   a) Immediate 'buy now' pages ❏
   b) An email follow-up series ❏
   c) Webinars ❏
   d) All of the above ❏

6. The website tracker of choice is:
   a) Google Analytics ❏
   b) Anything that you can get a hold of that costs money ❏
   c) Search and find the best for you ❏

7. The best way to get to know GA is:
   a) Use it ❏
   b) Use it a lot ❏
   c) Go through everything many times ❏
   d) Watch the video tutorials ❏
   e) All of the above ❏

8. When you find a page many are going to but are then leaving, what can you do?
   a) Spice it up a bit ❏
   b) Force your visitors to visit a new page with ninja mind tricks ❏
   c) Change your site completely ❏

9. When split testing:
   a) Test only one thing at a time ❏
   b) Test two entirely different pages each time ❏
   c) Change at least two things on the new page you are testing ❏

10. There is a point at which you can just stop testing and learning new things:
   a) True ❏
   b) False ❏

MONDAY

SEO: The backbone of any digital marketing strategy

Today we're going to be covering the first basic step of digital marketing and that is search engine optimization (SEO).

This is the solid base that, if you get it right, will help all your other areas of marketing.

Why?

Because just as digital marketing is a holistic (complete) approach to marketing in a primarily digital age, *SEO is also becoming more and more a holistic website experience for the user.*

If you want to sell online, you need to have a good website with good SEO backing this up.

SEO defined

SEO can be defined as the things you do for the pages on your website so that they are found by Google and to ensure that they show in the top ten results when people search for something related to your business.

For instance, this may include being found when your customers type the keywords 'chiropractor Dallas TX', 'dog grooming supplies' or 'cute kitten photos' (if that's what you're trying to make into a business) into Google.

This in turn brings you a lot of traffic and, depending on how valuable those keywords actually are, this can then in turn bring you new customers and clients.

So yes, this is pretty awesome but, as I will show later in the week, it is not the only way that your customers find their way to your door/website. Nor is it necessarily always the *best* way for your customers to come to you. In fact, depending on your market, it might not even be the best place to start.

But SEO is an essential skill to learn and it's not that difficult (regardless of what high-priced SEO consultants may lead you to believe) so let's get into it today, shall we?

So exactly how does SEO work?

People and SEO consultants have a million theories as to how exactly to go about doing this, but what really works?

I have written a whole book on this subject, which of course I recommend you read for more info, but here is the basic idea in a nutshell.

First look at it from Google's perspective: they want their results to be the best of any search engine, because the best results mean more users of their service, which means more eyeballs on their site and more eyeballs means that more users will click the paid ads on the right-hand side.

Google is continuously fine-tuning the number and types of factors they use to determine whether a page gets into the top ten results for a certain search phrase, like looking at how long people stay on your site, how fast your webpages load, the number of people who like and share your content on Facebook, Twitter or Google+ and so on.

But when you boil it all down, essentially what Google and the other search engines are looking for is a *great user experience*.

To sum it all up there are two aspects of your site that you need to keep in mind when developing it. If one is missing, you will not have the success you want out of your website in the long run.

First, you need to think about your on-site goals.

This means that your site should load quickly, look good and be logically laid out so people can find your content in the easiest and quickest manner possible.

Next, your site needs every page to be in some way related to your site's overall theme (e.g. dog product-related if you are selling dog products) and every page needs to be optimized for just one keyword phrase (more on this later).

Third, you need to take care of your off-page criteria.

If you have heard about SEO at all, you might have heard that getting high in Google is pretty much just about getting links.

And you'd be correct. However, the real power is by getting what are known as 'authority' links pointing to your pages and your website.

'Authorities' are websites and pages that Google deems highly trustworthy on your subject matter.

So for example, if you are a website selling accessories for iPods, iPads and iPhones, the ultimate (albeit unlikely) dream would be for Apple to link to you in some way.

But even if you're unable to get an 'Apple' level of authority linking to you, if enough people link to a page then that page will be seen by Google as an 'authority' on the subject and (all things being equal) they will move it up the rankings for certain keywords and search terms.

Although this extra 'weight' is not as high as it used to be, it is still there. However, if you want your site to *last* it is not all you should focus on.

Super ninja trick

Create your own 'authority' site. How can you do this? Create pages on something that Google sees as an 'authority' already!

The best site for this right now is YouTube and another one is Google+. There are a few others out there but these two are the most effective.

Create a business page on Google+ then post good YouTube videos using the same account. Send links to those videos and you will be amazed at the authority boost you will get now that these two authority pages are linking to you.

SEO guide

Now we know a bit more about SEO, what are you to do about it?

We see the search engines are looking for a great user experience. So what does this mean for you and your business?

Let me present to you 'Nick the geek's guide to solid SEO', the sure-fire steps to SEO that gives your website the best shot possible. (I can't guarantee anything though, since I don't own Google. I can dream though ...)

First step is your website's HTML code – the markup language used to build webpages – should be fully validated with W3C standards (speak to your techie about this).

Your website should load as fast as possible and should look good. It doesn't have to be the Sistine Chapel to start off but it shouldn't scare people away either and needs to have a good amount of content (at least ten optimized pages and five to ten optimized blog posts).

Load times can be improved by getting good-quality web hosting (it is definitely not all the same – drop me a line and I'll tell you who I use).

Keep your webpages' file sizes as small as possible to help load quickly and your images should also be optimized for the web (I tend to use JPGs wherever possible at 60 per cent compression – again, speak to your techie).

W3C compliance and load speed can both be covered by using a content management system like WordPress (free from WordPress.org) and getting a good premium theme from them that matches your business and goals (this will take care of the coding).

Premium themes average approximately $50 and will look like your website had thousands of dollars spent on it.

If you have a website already, go to http://webpagetest.org/ and test your site out for free (you want the load speed to be less than seven seconds to be good, fewer than five seconds to be the best).

Websites generally tend to have static, unchanging content on them, so to continually give Google and the other search engines a reason to keep visiting your website to index it in their huge databases, I recommend having a blog somewhere on your domain.

The search engines all tend to prefer new and timely content, so the more often new content is added to your site, the more the search engines will like it. And the more the search engines like it, the more often they'll add new pages from your site (your blog posts) into their databases and you then increase the chances of your website being shown to someone looking for what you offer.

More content = more chances to be found. Easy, isn't it?

SUNDAY
MONDAY
TUESDAY
WEDNESDAY
THURSDAY
FRIDAY
SATURDAY

Content

If your website was a building, then content is the foundation that makes that website go the distance.

Not just ordinary content but great content.

Why?

Because this is what your website visitors really want, they don't really care about your super-slick graphics, or your sci-fi looking interface. They want the answer to their question. They want information they can use.

If you give it to them, you will be rewarded by Google for it.

So not only do you want good content, you want good content that will match your ideal visitors' needs and desires. If you do it well, you will meet your visitors' needs and desires at a stage before they want to buy from you.

You also want, as much as possible, for *every* page of your site to be optimized for at least one keyword. Even if it is a keyword that is only searched 100 times a month. Every page should have some key phrase that you are trying to win for.

Definition

'Optimized' means the main keyword you'd like the webpage to rank for in Google.

So for example, let's say you want to target the keyword/search term 'Vietnamese dog brush'.

First of all, put the keyword as the filename (or the permalink if you're using a CMS) so it looks something like:

http://yourdomain.com/vietnamese-dog-brushes or
http://yourdomain.com/vietnamese-dog-brushes.html

You need the title of the page to use an H1 HTML tag (ask your techie) and contain your keyword within it but *not* be the exact keyword.

Something like 'high quality Vietnamese dog brushes'.

You should make sure that this 'close keyword' is mentioned first on the page, and once every 200 words or so in the content.

You should have at least one picture on the page that has a filename of the 'close keyword' and it is always good to have a video embedded on the page about the dog brush as well (more on this when we talk about YouTube later).

This requires a plan

First, do a bit of thinking about what your visitors want. This is key at this point; don't think about what *you would want* but what a *visitor wants*. These will often be two different things. You are the expert in this area (hopefully) and as such you have a lot more knowledge than your visitors.

For instance, say you are a chiropractor; you may search for 'chiropractor', while your prospective visitor may look for 'back pain specialist' or 'what to do to help a sore back'.

You will use acronyms and other jargon. For example, I would use SEO or PR (page rank), or '*ranking* a website' in my searching but you might use 'being found by Google' or 'online marketing' in yours.

Learn what this means for your potential customers and you will go somewhere many other experts in your field haven't gone.

Next, think about what your customers search for before they come to you. Looking for a chiropractor, maybe they will search for 'back pain home remedies'. Now, meeting this need may send some customers away (because the problem may be fixed), but those who find no relief or only some relief will now know who to visit for full professional help.

Say you make Facebook apps, maybe you can make a page on 'how to make a Facebook app'. People may be searching for them and a few will make their own app. But many of these just want to know the details and will then give you the money to do it for them because they can tell that you know what you are talking about.

Google Keyword Planner

Take these ideas for content and load them into the Google Keyword Planner tool. This will give you a bunch of additional ideas as it will spit out the related keywords to the phrases that you already have in mind.

What you are looking to get right now is both lower and higher demand. Look at the general search volume for the term. You should have a good mix of 100–500 per month and 1,000–5,000 per month related searches with which to begin your site (only do with less than this if you can afford to make fewer sales; if you make $1,000 per sale then you can live very well off of a 5 per cent conversion rate on 500 people).

What you *don't* want to do with your content

Don't go out and put random content on your site just because a lot of people are searching for it. If you go out and rank for, let's say, 'underwater hang-gliding' and you are a chiropractor, when people land on your site they're going to be understandably confused and will probably leave faster than you can say 'Jack Robinson'.

This is the equivalent of putting a huge '**Free sex**!' at the start of a newspaper ad and then saying 'Now I've got your attention ...' Don't do it.

What you *do* want to do with your content

Make your content high quality and every last word worth reading (or every last second worth watching if it's a video).
Some ideas for content:

- Videos – these are hugely advantageous when used creatively. Don't just post bland boring stuff; don't be afraid to show your fun side! Videos are great and can really drive people to your site (more on this later).
- Informative text content, ideally over 1,000 words long (Google likes more content on a page).
- High-quality images (like infographics) – use these as much as possible to explain what you do or an important aspect of your niche.

- Audio recordings – of you talking in a radio talk show format or interviews with other leading experts, and so on.
- Case studies of clients or customers that show their success with your product/service.

Next steps

Now you have a plan for your content, a well-designed and running site with a blog. The next step is to start getting people to the site (all the prettiness in the world won't make people visit).

One of the best ways to start doing this is going out and getting links that people click (more ideas later in the week!). But how to get these? They are actually embedded in the above content ideas.

For instance, if you create videos you can upload them to YouTube and as soon as you post them you should always put the link to your site as the first line in the video description and also encourage people to visit in the video.

If your videos are good, you will start getting clicks on this link and Google will quickly reward you for that.

This is a traffic source that I see many, many people surviving off **alone**. They don't even really need Google traffic. Though you should go after both of course!

When you do audio podcasts, you can then go out and submit your site to podcast directories, which in turn will link to your site and drive people back to your site.

When you interview an expert in your field, you'd better believe they will probably link back to you.

Building this way takes a bit of time and doesn't happen overnight but will build solid links and traffic that will last a lifetime if done right.

Another way to get links and traffic is to just be active in your niche reaching out to related businesses cross-promoting each other. This is particularly powerful for local businesses that require foot traffic to their door such as doctors.

In the case above, it wouldn't even have to be related so much as just another business in the area. Google sees those links almost as recommendations from friends.

Conclusion

I hope I didn't blow any brain cells with the above and if so I apologize (a little).

The bottom line is you need to take care of two things. First what is on your page (your on-page criteria). You need to make sure that the words that you want people to find your page with are in the right places on your site.

Secondly, you need to make sure that you are being linked to from good quality places out on the web (your off-page criteria) which will bolster your reputation in Google's eyes, rewarding you with improved rankings and, all things being equal, send you more visitors.

Summary

The following is a summary of what I suggested above in the SEO area:

1 Get a fast-loading well-designed site.
2 Create great content that your customers and potential customers will love, that meets a need they have (whether they know it now or not).
3 Become active in your niche (and area if you are a local business) and reach out to the established people around you to start getting links and traffic. Comment on other blogs in your niche (giving valuable insight) and leave your link.

That is it ...That is pretty much SEO. Tomorrow we will talk about the next traffic source – social media.

So now we have ten questions to help your head remember the important things you learned today:

SUNDAY
MONDAY
TUESDAY
WEDNESDAY
THURSDAY
FRIDAY
SATURDAY

Questions

1. SEO stands for:
a) Super epic organization ❏
b) Search engine optimization ❏
c) Send error out ❏
d) Search engine opposition ❏

2. Digital marketing is:
a) A holistic approach to marketing in a primarily digital age ❏
b) A great way to trick people into buying from you ❏
c) The ultimate way to make lots of money overnight ❏
d) Pure magic and impossible to learn ❏

3. SEO is:
a) A game where you learn to get one over on Google and get free traffic to your site ❏
b) The only way to get traffic to your site ❏
c) Becoming more and more a holistic website experience for the user and is only one of many ways to get traffic ❏
d) The be all and end all of digital marketing ❏

4. Keywords are:
a) Words shaped like a key ❏
b) Special magic words ❏
c) Words that you repeat three times and get traffic to your site ❏
d) The words that people type into Google/Yahoo to find your site ❏

5. There are two areas you need to keep in mind when you want to start getting traffic. These are:
a) Nice-looking websites and cool graphics ❏
b) The latest cutting-edge technology and a private server ❏
c) On-page and off-page criteria ❏
d) You should have done the Google rain dance and worn your lucky Google pin while turning around three times before sitting at your computer ❏

6. One key to reaching customers is:
a) Finding them after they have purchased from a competitor ❏
b) Reaching them before they even know they need your product/service ❏
c) Brainwashing them from birth to want your product ❏
d) Being really nice ❏

7. An optimized page is:
a) A page that looks nice ❏
b) A page that has been customized ❏
c) A page that has your keyword choice strategically put all over it (not too much though) ❏
d) A page made to trick the search engines into thinking that your page is perfect for that keyword ❏

8. You should optimize each page for how many keywords?
a) 1 ❏
b) 2 ❏
c) 3 ❏
d) 4 ❏

9. Great ideas for content are:
a) Interviews with related experts ❏
b) Videos ❏
c) Long articles (1,000 plus words) ❏
d) All of the above ❏

10. My recommendations for CMS and hosting are:
a) WordPress and a Cloud server on Hostgator ❏
b) Custom made and GoDaddy ❏
c) Custom made and a private server privately run ❏
d) None of the above ❏

SUNDAY

MONDAY

TUESDAY

WEDNESDAY

THURSDAY

FRIDAY

SATURDAY

TUESDAY

Social media marketing madness

Hi there and welcome to Tuesday! Hope yesterday was easy because today is going to get really tough ... just kidding!

I want to make this whole book as user-friendly as possible, which is why I don't get very technical and am trying on focus on the concepts that really work.

It's great to see you continuing to learn the tips and tricks to getting buyer traffic in this day and age and I actually have some particularly cool stuff today.

Today we are going to cover social media marketing or SMM for those who do this professionally. (What can I say? We love our acronyms.)

If SEO is a lot about your relationships within your marketplace (i.e. the related but-not-competing links that point at your site), then SMM is more about your relationship with your actual customers.

In fact, one of its primary and most effective uses for business is as an instant online customer support centre (more on this later).

What is social media?

Social media is defined as content that is generated and interacted with by the participants and the generators of said content.

To give you an example, say you take a picture (create content), you post it on Facebook (publish it on a social platform), a million people comment on it, like and share it with their friends.

You generated the content but the other participants interacted with it and in so doing spread it all over the world. In so doing, they became *content amplifiers*. This is one of the huge potential powers of social traffic.

They willingly spread your message and voice for you, amplifying what you could never have done at all on your own.

Now getting shared a million times is a rare thing (it's what you might have heard referred to as going 'viral').

But it can and does happen many times every single day.

However, that *shouldn't* be your goal for using social media because if it is you're going to be disappointed once you find out your funny cat video only got a hundred views (which is the YouTube average).

Why you need to be on social media

1 Your customers are there (*billions* of people around the world have a social presence of some kind on a social network).
2 See point 1. That is about it.

Seriously, don't give me anything about Facebook takes your identity or anything like that. If you are a business, you need to be where your clients and customers are, and you need to be interacting with them where they feel comfortable interacting.

So, now that that is out of the way ...

What different platforms are there?

There are literally hundreds of tiny social networks out there. Some exist just for small-business people or particular countries.

The main ones that you need to concern yourself with to start are:

- Facebook (I know big surprise right? Well it has over 1 billion users so it is a pretty big deal)
- YouTube (this is the second most searched site in the world, making it the second biggest search engine in the world and is also Google-owned)
- LinkedIn (particularly good for business-to-business operations but also good for any business as a place to be found by other business people that may just want your service or you might want to use theirs)
- Google+ (not only good for social traffic, also has some SEO benefits that will be talked about later today)
- Twitter (more specialized but still very useful)
- Pinterest (a new up-and-coming social platform that is fast gaining popularity and value)
- Instagram (an image- and video-based social network popular with the tech-savvy demographic because it's a smartphone app)

If you only could choose three to start, I would choose Facebook, YouTube and Google+ for the normal business; for the business-to-business company, replace Facebook with LinkedIn.

Now let us determine what SMM is good for and what it isn't good for so you can start to have an idea about how you can use it for your own business.

What social media is good for

1 Social media is a great place to interact with your customers on a personal level.

   They can be made to feel comfortable posting questions on your timeline or as comments to updates you've posted.

   On Twitter, the tagline is 'It is all about the conversation' and that is the truth, not only on Twitter but on Facebook, YouTube and all the other social platforms out there.

   If you ship products as part of your business, you can be sure to get a few 'where is my package?' Facebook page posts now and then. As well as other product-related questions ...

> ## Note:
>
> Always, and I mean always, answer these questions publicly (whether they are bad or good). If you do not, nothing can stop your other customers from interacting with you faster.
>
> It is really a bummer to go on a fan page and one of the first posts is, 'Where the heck is my package? I ordered it 5 weeks ago!' and the post is weeks old and there is absolutely no response from the page owner ...
>
> The least they could do is take five seconds and go on their page and delete the comment. But no it just sits there scaring away prospect after prospect whether the page owner knows it or not.
>
> The question is still there so as far as the person from the outside looking in knows this business owner never checks their Facebook page so why should they check it?

2 Social media is also a great place to get social proof.

   Everyone always goes where the crowd is just to see what they are looking at.

   It's the same for your social efforts; build up your fan base and more people will follow, just to see what is going on, and they may also end up being customers.

3 Social media is good for lead generation (prospecting).

This is not to say that social media is good at direct selling (see number 1 in the next section) but it is a great place to find people who are willing to find out more about you before buying.

4 Social media is great for product demonstrations and service descriptions.

This is where YouTube shines and, by extension, provides something you can share on Facebook and Twitter, that is, the ability to demonstrate how something works and explain it in detail. Whether this is the latest do-hickey that you came up with or how a divorce settlement really works, this is a good place and way to illustrate it and make it clear for people to understand.

What social media is *not* good at

The number 1, and I repeat, the number 1 thing you need to know about social media is that it is not a good place for:

1 Selling directly and incessantly

As you can imagine, I'm on one social media platform or another pretty much constantly and the one thing I continually see is businesses that do nothing but broadcast their latest promotion ... **all the time**!

I mean, this is alright if you're a deals site like Groupon or something like that. But if you're not, you're just going to turn your prospects off and then you've lost them for good (if you're lucky); if you're not lucky you'll get your account banned for spamming.

Just the other day I saw someone in a £185/month private Facebook mastermind group spam twice within an hour with their first two ever posts. Crazy.

No one likes to be sold to while hanging out with their friends.

That is what you are doing if you do nothing but broadcast sales messages and nothing will banish you to social oblivion faster as well.

So don't do it.

Now, thinking about the above scenario, say you became friends with a member of the staff of a company and one day they suggested to you, 'Come check out this sale my company is having'.

That is a completely different matter.

So the occasional sales message combined with good interaction skills is all right.

Just for heaven's sake don't do it all the time! Try to limit it to once a month, if at all.

2 Social media is not a place for blah content

You have to excite your users the second they lay eyes on your post.

You want them to be hitting the share button before they even know what they are doing because what you share is that cool.

They don't want the latest blah article you found via Google search. They definitely don't care about your tenth anniversary of being in business ... Really they don't care ... Seriously ...

TIP

Super ninja trick

Take what your customers don't care abut and make them care about it.

What do your customers care about? They care about what is in it for them or how their lives are affected or can be improved.

So to turn around the ten year anniversary of your business say 'We are celebrating giving dogs the best cuts in the New York area for the last ten years' - make them care!

Lead with why they should care and they will do just that.

How to get started

Go to all of the sites above and register your unique name (whether you plan on using them immediately or not).

Otherwise, you may find that the name you want is gone before you get there.

Next, choose your starting three (for this example, I will use Facebook, YouTube and Pinterest as Facebook/Google+/LinkedIn are similar).

Facebook

For Facebook, LinkedIn and Google+ (G+), you first have to get a personal account before you can register your business name and get yourself a page for your business.

I recommend that if you already have a personal account then great, go ahead and create a business page. See the links below for help with this.

http://lk.gs/fbpages (How to create Pages on Facebook)

http://lk.gs/gpluspages (How to create Pages on G+)
http://lk.gs/lipages (How to create Pages on LinkedIn)

Next you need to populate all three of these pages with as much useful information and content as possible.

No one likes walking into a ghost town page with just a headline and an 'under construction' sign.

If you are a business with any history whatsoever, it should be relatively easy for you to create content here.

Put it all down in chronological order. (They all let you do this.)

For instance, put in when certain products became available, any awards you have received, any conventions you have been too, major partnerships you have started and so on.

Anything that just shows you are a real company. Photos. Videos. Audio. Scans of newspaper clippings. Anything.

Done well, this will have your potential customer scrolling through your history thinking 'this is one accomplished company'.

Note:

Don't make stuff up. Nothing can be worse than lying on social media. You **will** be found out. A good word travels at light speed, a bad word at warp speed!

If you're a new company, that doesn't mean you don't put up information, but put up information about your planned ventures, and your accomplishments so far. Even if it is only joining your local chamber of commerce and hiring some cool people at the local job fair.

Be real and share your company's life (if ever so short) there.

Now get some fans. I recommend getting all your employees and their family, your family (even the mother-in-law if you dare) and past/current clients and customers to like your page on Facebook.

Then, run a short 'like' campaign using Facebook Pay Per Click Adverts targeting people within your local area who might be familiar with your company. Aim to get more than 25 likes as this will give you the ability to choose a 'vanity' URL for your page.

Something like: facebook.com/dog-supplies-inc.

It will also show that you are a happening place and moving and grooving company, at least in people's minds at this point. Now you need to start producing content.

> ## Note:
> LinkedIn and G+ are different in the way you get to know people, join and create 'groups' related to your business and start posting good content.
>
> It won't take much to have effect in those places.

Producing great content on Facebook

Creating good content on Facebook is not as difficult as it may seem but it can be a case of trial and error depending on your customers.

So how to really make good content?

Think emotional.

What gets your customers/clients emotional? Not just nice, but in an emotional moment. Do you have a pet service? Maybe some pictures of kittens ...

For instance, a day-care centre could post pictures of cute kids, have inspirational stories of parenthood, money-saving deals you've found on clothes, toiletries and so on.

Maybe, though you don't have such a specific group of people, you still have a group of people. Like teenagers or young adults. What gets them excited and emotional? (Teenage boys of course don't get 'emotional'–'stoked' or 'blown away' maybe ...)

Those are the things you need to think of to make great content on social networks that get shared over and over again.

Your latest doo-hickey to get Fluffy's hair straight will get trumped *every* single time by that picture of a dog and cat snuggling together with 'friends forever' written underneath it.

The more that people read and share your emotion-inciting posts, the more people will remember you and see your other posts later when you mention a sale that you have just for your Facebook friends.

That being said, the three best formats for getting an emotional response for the most part are:

- pictures/other images
- videos
- everything else.

See, a picture is really worth a thousand words.

Producing great content on other social networks

For G+, you should do the same emotion-impacting things that you put on your Facebook page. But LinkedIn is a different animal. The content that needs to be talked about there needs to show people your company and you contributing in big ways to the community as a whole.

You need to start groups and contribute good content to related groups.

For example, if you are a lawyer consider starting a group in your area of expertise to answer people's questions, then *really* answer people's questions.

Many businesses start these things but then promptly forget that they did and get 'too busy'. If you want to see growth on LinkedIn, you need to be willing to contribute to the conversation.

If you aren't able to find time, consider outsourcing (covered later).

YouTube content creation

Here you need to be creating things that your customers are looking for and that really depends on your market.

'How to' videos may really work for you here or instructional videos on how to use your products. Other things that help are to create videos that talk about things that people would look for before coming to you. Perhaps 'back pain remedies' if you are a chiropractor or 'how to fill out small claims forms in your state' if you are a lawyer. Almost any business can profit from this kind of advertising, because almost everything can be portrayed by a good video.

There are some rules.

Set and follow a set flow with every video. Here is my suggested flow:

1 Introduction with music and logo with brief intro to yourself
2 Then tell them what you are going to explain/do
3 Explain/do it
4 Sum it all up with a conclusion
5 Put a call to action (Visit your site, download your report, etc.)
6 Don't be boring
7 Don't be boring
8 Don't be boring

That is about it, be yourself (unless you are boring); in that case find someone else that can show enthusiasm. I am currently working with a client who is not a naturally exciting individual, so I asked him to actually put his employee in the videos.

Don't take it personally, it is how it is. You need to show excitement or people will think you are in it only for the money (which may be the case but don't *show* them that).

It will be trial and error, at least to start with, to find the content that people want but here is a secret to success.

After producing your first ten videos, which will establish you as an expert, you can ask your viewers what they want you to talk about.

Do those things, then ask again, 'Now what do you want me to talk about?'

Some of the best YouTubers never have to 'figure out what to do' because all they do is ask their viewers what they want and give it to them.

You must remember this is a two-way street, you are not just broadcasting these videos (or those pictures on Facebook) to faceless millions. You are broadcasting them to specific people that have an interest in you and your company.

If you ask them what they want, they will probably tell you (unless you are producing such boring content at that point that they might not even be seeing your requests). Maybe you only get a few responses to your first request. Do them and you will win the business of those who requested them.

Then, when people see that you are listening, more people will speak up next time.

Success is never instant on social media. You need real people talking about you to get other real people to come.

Why you need to be on Google+

You may have noticed that Google+ (G+) is in all of my recommendations and you might wonder why. If you track these things at all, you might know that there is not necessarily as big an audience there as there is at Facebook.

Well there is one reason and that is SEO.

Here is one of the places that SEO and social media intersect. The only reason that there is SEO is because of Google. Google is 63 per cent of the US market and 90 per cent plus of all the other markets.

Here is an example.

A little while ago I had a website where I posted a link on my G+ to a site that I own in Brazil. Recently doing a search for that term on Google, I realized that my comment for that link is *above* the actual site itself!

This is just part of the power of G+ though. You need to realize that G+ has the potential to be a real authority builder and a way for Google to 'verify' your identity, so to speak.

They give you a bit of code now that means if you post on any site you own, you can link back to your G+ profile and get 'credit' for that post even if it isn't on your site.

This has huge potential as now Google has to do a lot less guess work and will start seeing you as a real authority the more you do this, with your site and other authority sites in your niche.

Being on G+ is also essential for your local profile in that Google Local is now rolled up in your G+ business profile.

So all you need is one personal G+ account, one business G+ page and, optionally, one personal G+ page. When Google sees that you are linking to your website and other sites, it will credit you for posts there and it therefore becomes one big SEO feedback loop.

The extra visitors from social media will just be icing on the cake.

More advanced image tips

As I showed above, images are the number one thing being posted to Facebook at this time.

Now the best way to put images on social networks is to put images on two other specific networks at the same time.

These were not recommended above because it is usually best not to bite off more than you can chew to start with and posting images on Facebook alone is just fine if you want to test the waters.

To do images right and get the maximum exposure for your image efforts, post them both on Instagram and Pinterest at the same time.

Pinterest is mostly aimed at the desktop crowd (though there are many mobile users) and Instagram is almost completely aimed at the mobile crowd. In fact, without a mobile device you can't really use Instagram properly. You can view images using sites like:

http://web.stagram.com (Webstagram)
http://statigr.am/ (Statigram)

However, you can upload any photos you have to Instagram by simply emailing them to your phone email address or putting them on an SD card and putting them on your phone and/or tablet.

So after you have tested out your images on Facebook, head
over to Instagram and Pinterest and get to gramming and
pinning. They are truly a match made in heaven.

Summary

Be real and interactive on your social media accounts and post things that people get emotionally involved with and you will be light years ahead of your competition.

Focus on not being boring and check your updates constantly. If you don't hire someone to be doing it on a constant basis, there are many places online like oDesk.com where you can find people who will do it for a reasonable low monthly fee (say $200).

Be involved in as many platforms as possible from Facebook to YouTube and everything in between. This gives your customers multiple ways to interact with you and also gives you authority in Google's eyes.

Be sure to include getting on Google+; whether you actually get traffic itself, this more then anything else can get your business noticed by Google and can get you listed in two spots on the first page of Google if you do it right.

SUNDAY
MONDAY
TUESDAY
WEDNESDAY
THURSDAY
FRIDAY
SATURDAY

Big things now include images and videos but mostly images are king now. The latest updates Facebook just made increase the up front and centre position that Facebook was already giving images.

So images are not going away anytime soon.

Oodles of questions for your noodle:

Questions

1. SMM stands for:
a) Super Monday madness ❏
b) Sonic music monotone ❏
c) Social media marketing ❏
d) Social money mayhem ❏

2. One of the main uses for social media is:
a) To make massive amounts of money from people who trip over themselves to buy in your sales ❏
b) To be a customer support centre ❏
c) To build an email list ❏
d) Both b and c are correct ❏

3. Social media is:
a) All websites in the world ❏
b) Sites where users and creators interact seamlessly ❏
c) Only Facebook ❏
d) Only special sites named social media ❏

4. The main social sites are:
a) Facebook ❏
b) YouTube ❏
c) LinkedIn ❏
d) Pinterest ❏
e) Google+ ❏
f) Twitter ❏
g) All of the above ❏

5. Social media is ideal for direct sales:
a) True ❏
b) False ❏

6. Social media is a great place for social proof:
a) True ❏
b) False ❏

7. The best type of social content is:
a) Lots of related articles every day ❏
b) Pictures ❏
c) Videos ❏
d) Emotionally moving pictures ❏

8. Google+ is ideal for:
a) Social and SEO ❏
b) SEO only ❏
c) Social, SEO, and 'author rank' ❏
d) None of the above ❏

9. After expanding in your top three networks:
a) Stop there and keep going ❏
b) Move on to Pinterest and Instagram ❏
c) Go really deep to niche-specific ❏
d) Work on the hundreds of other social networks out there ❏

10. The most important thing is to be 'Real'!
a) True ❏
b) False ❏

WEDNESDAY

Pay per click (PPC) simplified and explained

Today we are going to discuss another tool that should be in every digital marketer's toolkit and that is pay per click (PPC) marketing.

SEO and social media are great ways to get traffic for 'free' – although not totally 100 per cent free because you're spending time that not all business people have to spare to be able to create content, get links, likes and shares and so on from your marketplace.

Sometimes it is nice just to click a couple of buttons and get visitors and this is exactly what PPC can do for you, but only if you do it right.

Don't go crazy now and say I told you PPC is a magic button to make money online. Far be it from me to say such a thing. What PPC can do is make money on demand if you do it right. This, like anything, requires work plus knowledge and analytical ability to read numbers, and then you need to apply those numbers.

First, let's talk about the state of the PPC market and then get into how to do it right.

PPC ads in a nutshell

It should come as no surprise that Google is number one in this arena. Google's AdWords (PPC) system is the primary revenue stream for Google ($42.5 billion in 2012) – well, at least until driverless cars and Google Glass launch.

Facebook is Google's next major competitor in the PPC space but their revenue is just a tenth of Google's and uses a different system (which I personally think is better) that we will get into later in this section.

And also you have the smaller players like Yahoo Search Marketing, and Bing PPC that all have their place.

Google search ads

When someone types in keywords, the first two to three listings are ads as well as all the links on the right side of the page.

This is Google's Search Network.

You can see a sample screenshot of those ads below in the highlighted boxes:

Also Google has its tentacles (shh don't tell them I said that, I mean its ads) on millions of websites across the web.

This is known as Google's Display Network. Website owners can apply to Google to have these ads on their websites via their AdSense Program and this is a legitimate way to help monetize a website.

You can learn more about Google's Ad Networks here: http://adwords.google.com

So how does PPC marketing work?

There are two main types of PPC – keyword related and demographically related.

Keyword related is how Google does it in their Search Network.

You bid on which keywords (search terms) your ad will show up on the right-hand side of and you pay $x.xx or just $.xx every time your advert is clicked.

You can find out the average cost per click (CPC) for each keyword using either the Google Keyword Planner or Google's Traffic Estimator tool (accessible only from within a paid AdWords account).

The price you pay is a combination of the amount of competition for the keyword and how popular your ad is. The more times your ad is clicked in your PPC campaign, the more Google rewards you by ever so slowly nudging you up the paid ad rankings.

So if your ad was initially placed fourth and ended up getting more clicks than the third, second and first place ads, it's possible that your ad will jump the queue into first place and you'll still be paying the same amount as you were when you were in fourth place.

Once again, Google rewards relevancy with ranking, and because ads in first place generally get more clicks than lower-positioned ads (assuming it does get the clicks), you'll end up sending more traffic to your website at a lower cost than your competitors!

Google's Display Network

This is a bit different from the Search Network for two reasons:

First, with the Search Network you're limited to only using text ads. But because the Display Network is made up of external websites, you can use a text ad, a banner image ad or a video ad.

Second, you don't bid on keywords shown up from a search; instead you bid to show your ad on pages Google deems relevant to a keyword.

And with the Display Network, you can either pay CPC or CPM. CPM is Cost Per Mille, the cost per 1,000 impressions. So when Google shows your ad 1,000 times, you pay $x.xx regardless of whether your ads are clicked or not.

Facebook ads

Facebook does both PPC and CPM but they are demographic-based. Their PPC network used to only work inside of Facebook, but at the time of writing they are in the process of setting up their own 'Display Network' to compete with Google where Facebook ads show up directly on external websites.

You can already run 'retargeting' campaigns with Facebook, where each new visitor to a website gets a small file called a 'cookie' placed in their browser enabling the website to show their ads on other websites in the same network, Facebook Exchange (FBX).

And because Facebook's PPC network is 'demographic-based', this means that instead of targeting what people are *searching* for, you can target people according to *who they are*, for instance, the things they like, their occupation, their age, their sex and so on.

Although you can do this type of demographic targeting in Google, it's nowhere near as detailed as it is in Facebook, because Google simply doesn't have the data. This might possibly be another reason why Google+ was created. Maybe, just maybe ...

The problem is that some people don't even know that Facebook has ads. I mentioned to my Mum recently I was running ads on Facebook and she said, 'Really, do they have those? Where are they?' Ad blindness strikes ...

The others

I have tried Yahoo/Bing ads that follow pretty much the same rules as Google as well as other small players, and I'm not very impressed by them or their conversion rates although Yahoo/Bing was OK (your mileage may vary).

Facebook and Google are where you should focus your effort if you choose this path. You want to reach as many people as quickly as possible with this method, so go with the big boys first. So why would you choose this path? Let's look at the pros and cons.

Pros

You know that people are at least vaguely interested in what you have.

They went and clicked your ad so they must be at least curious to see what is on the other side (if you wrote your ad right, that is, more on this later).

You can really focus down to the nitty-gritty for your visitors.

If you want people from North Dakota who like bubble gum and rock and roll, you can definitely find them with Facebook, not quite in such detail as with Google, though you could find people that are searching for particular terms around rock and roll or bubble gum, just not both in the same campaign.

You can say with (almost) certainty that you will get traffic.

When they're on the ball, both Google and Facebook can approve an ad very quickly – I've personally had ads approved and live in less than ten minutes before but it's normally within an hour or two.

Cons

Costs per click (CPC) are rising generally and can be unnaturally high unless you do proper research, choose your correct keywords or demographics and also point ads to a specific page on your site, not your homepage.

Both Facebook and Google are now public companies, answering to shareholders and having to go out of their way to make sure that they are profitable.

And that means extracting as much money as possible from advertisers.

CPCs can range from anywhere between 5 cents to 50 dollars *a click* and sometimes more. It all depends on the market and keywords being bid on. So you really have to do your research into every word you are bidding for to make sure that you are getting the amount you can afford.

Even this can get really expensive really fast.

Luckily, both Google and Facebook allow you to set daily budgets that you cannot go over, so you shouldn't have to sell a kidney or your first born to pay your PPC bill.

But that daily limit needs to take into account the number of clicks you want, clicks sending people to your website.

Slight aside

PPC works really well, especially if you're doing any type of testing as you can find out pretty quickly what is working.

You need to keep in your mind though that you should aim to generate at least 200 visitors a day to your test URLs so you can be reasonably sure which item you're testing is the winner.

Here's a great online calculator that will help to tell you whether your testing results are statistically significant:

http://lk.gs/significant

Also make sure that you set your daily budget high enough so you can get at least 200 daily visitors.

PPC requires a lot of research and tracking

Some keywords may be expensive but might end up converting less well than other cheaper keywords for you or vice-versa.

So you need to do research combined with a lot of tracking. Tracking is where you see where the traffic is coming from and how well it converts (how many people do what you want them to). Compare the keywords to other keywords and narrow down exactly what you need.

Both Facebook and Google have free tools that will allow you to track sales, leads or other outcomes and so on.

That is the list of pros and cons. Now you may wonder why anyone would go through the hassle. When would it be a good idea to do PPC?

When to do PPC

First when **not** to do it (so we get it out of the way): don't ever do PPC just to get visitors to your homepage. You need a real reason and purpose for your visitors to put together any kind of PPC campaign that has any sort of effectiveness because you need to know exactly how much is going out and how much is coming in. Here is my list of services and products to sell via PPC (along with some exceptions).

Subscription services

One situation is if you have a product that is a monthly paid subscription, a service to which customers will be loyal or is a high converting high-ticket item that you don't spend a lot of money to get.

For instance, say you are an online service writing press releases for companies. You have a monthly service that releases a certain amount per month or you know that, when you write for companies, they tend to stick with you because you do such a good job. Either way, depending on how much you charge, you now have an idea how much you can afford to spend to get one customer (this is called the client lifetime value).

So if you charge £49.95 a month for your subscription and you know that on average a customer will stay with you for 12 months, then the lifetime value of that customer is 12 × £49.95 = £599.40.

Why is this important? When you know how much each customer is worth to you, you can figure out how much you're prepared to spend to acquire each new customer.

If you're just starting out with a new business and website, you won't have this initial data, so just concentrate on coming up with a compelling offer with a great price, make a great looking site, and direct traffic to a landing page that presents your offer well (more on this in the next section about landing pages), and see whether anyone is interested enough to buy.

Keep track of your results and as you discover over time how long customers stay with you, you'll be able to gradually increase your spending to acquire new customers.

Big ticket items

The next area this could help with is if you have a big ticket item, which could be consulting of some sort or even a high-ticket physical item, like a swimming pool. Either way, let's imagine the item is priced at $5,000.

If it costs you $1 per click to get people to your sales page and if one out of every 500 buys what you're offering (which is an awful conversion rate, but still) it might have cost you $500 to get that new customer, but you still made $4,500 gross profit and you now have that person in your customer database to sell more to down the line and maybe get referrals so more caching!

Social experimentation

Another place it could work in the short term is getting people's opinions.

For instance, say you are writing a book and you want to know if people are interested in your subject of hang-gliding in the Andes mountains. You put together a little $50 campaign that has hang-gliding and Andes mountain-related keywords with its title, 'Hang-glide the Andes mountains?' You can then judge by how readily people click on the ad whether they are interested or not.

Expert marketing tip alert
You could also put on the landing page a place for people to ask their most burning question about hang-gliding in the Andes mountains and now you know exactly what people will want to see in your book (that isn't even ready yet) and you'll have a list of people to email when your book is ready for a quick burst of sales.

The same theory applies to product retailers and service providers. If people often ask the same questions before they purchase what you're offering, put up a Frequently Asked Questions page answering them.

Book titles

This tip can also work if you are writing a book and are wondering what the most effective title is. Take the best ones you have come up with, put them together on a landing page and send people via Facebook or Google PPC to vote on the title they like best.

You could also have them enter their email address to get the results and also add them to an 'early bird' notification list where you give them a substantial discount (or even a free copy) as a thank you.

Getting subscribers

One other place you can use PPC is for a small niche product to get subscribers to your email newsletter.

This is where you can really use the fact that you are a small site to your advantage. I heard about someone who once did a small Facebook PPC campaign to their niche bulldog website. It had one focus, getting newsletter subscribers; they spent $20 but ended up with 100 subscribers, several comments on how nice their site was and even a couple of sales.

Likes to Facebook fanpages

As said earlier in the social media section, it is sometimes good to get those first few fans with a quick campaign targeting people that will be interested in your page in the first place.

I've done this very successfully with many, many fanpages. On one video-game related fanpage, I've added nearly 200,000 fans in just a couple of months for less than $200. (For more social media strategies see below.)

PPC advertising strategies

So now you have a focus, how do you set up your campaigns?

First you *need* to watch the relevant tutorial videos provided by Google and Bing to show you the *mechanics* of creating campaigns and ad groups:

http://google.com/adwords/onlineclassroom
http://advertise.bingads.microsoft.com/en-us/new-to-search-marketing

(Click the Getting Started tab on Bing for even more video tutorials.)

Now you've watched them, let's talk about structuring PPC ad campaigns on the Google and Bing search networks.

The most common way is to use the 'long tail keyword' approach by creating multiple ad groups, each revolving around a main root keyword and having similar keywords in the same group.

If we go back to the dog grooming example we used previously, and I type the keyword 'dog grooming' into Google's Keyword Tool, I get a series of keywords all grouped together by theme like:

KIT:
dog grooming kit
dog grooming kits
grooming kits for dogs
dog grooming kits for sale
dog grooming starter kit

TUBS:
dog grooming tubs
dog grooming tub
dog grooming bath tubs
dog wash tub
dog grooming tubs for sale
used dog grooming tubs
dog bath tub
dog grooming baths

CLIPPERS:
dog grooming clippers
best dog grooming clippers
dog grooming clippers reviews
wahl dog grooming clippers
clippers for dog grooming
dog grooming clippers australia
best dog clippers
dog grooming clippers for sale
clippers dog grooming
dog grooming clippers uk
Plus a lot more ...

Once you've selected the keywords and ad groups you want to use, you can transfer them into an existing campaign in your Google AdWords account (if you're already logged in) with a couple of mouse clicks by selecting the Add To Account button.

Bing doesn't use quite as refined a process as Google so what I generally do is to use the exact same keywords and ad grouping in Bing.

If you use the free Google AdWords Editor and Bing Ads Editor software programs, you can easily export your Google campaigns and import them into Bing quickly and easily.

Just search in Google for 'Bing Ads Editor' and 'Google AdWords Editor' to get the download links for your country.

Some quick dos and don'ts.

Do:

- Set a daily amount you can afford even if it doesn't convert at all.
- Have an open mind and test out different headlines and bodies of your ads and see which work out and which don't (this could be the exact opposite of what you think will happen sometimes).
- Try and focus on the *exact* keywords that you want to get clicks on. The more specific these are, the cheaper and more effective the click becomes.
- Wherever possible, point an ad to a landing page on your website that is related to your ad.
- Always try to get at least an email address for your efforts.
- Follow the search engine or social network's guidelines to the letter.

Don't:

- Make the click go to a one-page website. This will never be approved by Google, Bing or Facebook. Instead have it focused on a landing page somewhere in your site where the focus is what you want the visitor to do.
- Try to get clicks so that you can send the visitor to a page where you try and get them to click another ad. This is known as 'arbitrage' and sooner or later you will end up having your account banned.

- Make low-quality landing pages that are not directly relevant to the ad text. For more information on best practices for landing pages, refer to this guide by Google: http://bit.ly/ReH2nd.
- Write headlines or body that is written just to get clicks. Clicks is not the point; the point is to get people that are already interested in what they will get on the other side.

PPC strategies for Facebook

As I mentioned before, Facebook is a different beast because there are no keywords as such to bid to show your ad for.

Instead, you need to target people interested in related subjects, located in a certain geographic area, by the college or university they went to, their sex or any other combinations of demographic information.

Based upon my own experiences with Facebook PPC, here's how I recommend you structure your campaigns.

Where possible, link your ads to a Facebook page. People don't really like it when you take them outside of Facebook. In my tests, the costs per click of my campaigns halved when I sent people to a Facebook page instead of an external URL.

If you intend to run a PPC campaign to generate likes for your company's Facebook page, also consider creating a Facebook page for a celebrity or subject that has a broad appeal and is somehow related to your product or service *and then* running a PPC campaign to generate likes for *that* page too.

For example, if you were a weight loss consultant who specializes in helping women lose weight and get fit, you might create a fanpage around a female celebrity who has successfully lost weight and now looks great, for instance Jennifer Hudson if you're in the US or maybe Davina McCall if you're in the UK.

Piggy-backing on a celebrity or broad subject like 'weight loss' should make it easier to generate likes for *that* page, targeting people using your criteria (local area, sex, age, etc.) and then you can send occasional 'promoted posts' to your fans with special offers on your company Facebook page.

Boomerang Ninja PPC Trick

This is a technique that few marketers will share with you because it is so powerful and that is retargeting or what I like to call 'boomerang ninja marketing'.

What this means is that if someone visits your site they are automatically given a little code and when they go other sites on the web they will start seeing your display ads. This can be on everywhere from other Google sites, on Facebook, as well as Yahoo.

As give or take 98 per cent of those people that visit your website through social media/SEO and PPC will not actually buy, this means that those potential customers will now have a chance to come back when they are ready to buy without having to actually remember your website's name.

This tool is Ninja-like in that, whether consciously or unconsciously, your visitors suddenly start seeing your ads at their favourite web news site and the sites they visit every day like Facebook.

This causes them to slowly but surely begin to trust you more and more and see you as an authority if only because they saw your ad on the New York Times website ...

The services I use for this are:

http://adroll.com.
http://perfectaudience.com

Both of these offer simple and elegant solutions and reach a lot of websites around the world.

Video PPV on YouTube and Facebook (the next big thing?)

As I have stated in other places in this book, YouTube is the second biggest search engine in the world and it is totally worth your time to create videos to get traffic. Now though, with their new pay-per-view program (PPV), they have become even more potent.

Say you create a video but you are wondering if it converts real fast.

Spend $20 and get a bunch of views to it and see!

Out of those views, how many clicked through to your page? How many of those became customers?

At this point you might want to optimize it more and edit it a bit. With YouTube's average view time, you can see where people start to drop off and it might give you an idea of what to change.

Or it might make sense to leave the ad up and continue to pay for views.

Otherwise, if it still converts and retains your audience but not enough to make sense continuing the ads, just keep it up on YouTube and get natural views.

Either way it is a win-win for you by saving time and helping you improve at the same time.

Once you get a few good videos converting well on YouTube, consider setting up a campaign on Facebook as well, driving dirt-cheap clicks to these.

This way you can get multiple uses out of your successes.

Ninja tip:

When a potential customer watches a video, they become an 'educated prospect', that is, they know about you, what you do and what problem your product solves.

They will still not convert 100 per cent but some studies have shown educated prospects to be worth 10 times what an uneducated click is worth.

Now combine this with the boomerang marketing technique detailed in the section before this (targeted just to those educated prospects that land on that page) and you may just have an unstoppable PPC force!

Summary

PPC can be done on the cheap or it can be expensive if you don't have a specific goal. Either way if you keep the focus right you can make it profitable.

The key is to make everything measurable. If it's not measurable you are spending money without any idea of whether you're making a profit or losing your shirt.

Focus on your keywords and get ads that get clicks and make sales. Once you determine those and get your percentages, you can pour money into them as you know how much you can afford to spend to get one person to buy.

Then you can branch out and start experimenting with different keywords where the return is not so guaranteed.

And on and on it goes.

Experiment – do 'split tests' (i.e. run two different landing pages targeting the same keyword and see which does better).

SUNDAY
MONDAY
TUESDAY
WEDNESDAY
THURSDAY
FRIDAY
SATURDAY

Test run 'boomerang' (retargeting) ads and definitely give video PPV marketing a spin (huge potential).

In everything start small (100–1000 clicks/ views) and make sure it is profitable before you commit your life savings to the Google gods.

Questions

1. PPC stands for:
a) Perfectly politically correct ❏
b) Payment potentially considered ❏
c) Pay per click ❏
d) Panning people consolidated ❏

2. The main PPC giants are:
a) Facebook ❏
b) Google ❏
c) YouTube ❏
d) Bing ❏
e) Everybody else ❏
f) Both a, b, and c ❏

3. Be sure to place a daily limit based on:
a) How much you expect to make ❏
b) The size of the market ❏
c) How much you can afford to completely lose ❏

4. Subscription services:
a) Are a good service to use PPC to get clients ❏
b) Are a bad idea to drive PPC traffic to ❏
c) May or may not work ❏

5. Your homepage:
a) Is a good page to use PPC to get clients ❏
b) Is a bad idea to drive PPC traffic to ❏
c) May or may not work ❏

6. When you do PPC, it is good to have the focus of those clicks to be:
a) Four different options ❏
b) Three different options ❏
c) Two different options ❏
d) One measurable thing that you want them to do ❏

7. Before you start some PPC campaigns, you should know:
a) Your lifetime client value ❏
b) How much you are willing to spend ❏
c) What you want the click to do ❏
d) Have a plan for what to do with the information you are going to glean ❏
e) All of the above ❏

8. Always try in your PPC campaign to:
a) Make sales for your efforts ❏
b) Learn everything about your clients for your efforts ❏
c) Get at least an email address for your efforts ❏

9. Landing pages are:
a) Where the potential client 'lands' after clicking on your ad ❏
b) One-page sites that your clients want to visit ❏
c) Only for users of private planes ❏

10. Retargeting ads mean:
a) Someone visiting your website will now see targeted ads on other pages ❏
b) You will know where they live to set up your sniper nest ❏
c) You can now find out everything about this person ❏
d) b and c are correct ❏

THURSDAY

Mobile optimization and getting mobile users

You cannot miss this, the internet world is changing and it is changing quickly. Times are changing so fast, that today is the day you need to make the changes I am going to be talking about.

This is not something to do next month, this is not something to put off till you have time. This is something that you must do if you want to have a digital marketing business at all.

What is this essential bit of tech?

Mobile technology

I'll give you some stats to back up my statement above in a minute, first though, what are the immediate steps you need to take today?

Making your website ready for the mobile generation

First, your website needs to be ready for mobile users. (Yeah great, thanks Captain Obvious!)

Sounds stupid, but according to one survey by Adobe and E-consultancy, just 45 per cent of marketers polled have a mobile-optimized website.

My personal feeling is that this figure is actually much lower but I don't have any data to back this up, it's just a hunch from the many websites I have visited; many of those that think their website is ready probably don't know what 'mobile optimized' means.

Regardless, if you're optimized for mobile your **whole business** will gain a *huge* advantage over your competition just for being first in line for mobile users.

Now you need to know some numbers to get this into perspective and understand why I sound so serious.

Currently there are 2.4 billion internet users worldwide.

When it comes to growth, the most is now happening outside the West. China, in the last four years, added more internet users then there are people in the USA.

But the internet penetration of the USA still stands at an all-time high of 78 per cent, while China is only at 40 per cent at this point.

What does this mean?

This means that the internet is still growing, and still has plenty of space to grow further, being only about 25 per cent of the total population on the planet.

This also means that having international visitors will become more and more commonplace.

Great but what does this mean to you as a small business in Bithlo, Florida?

What you need to focus on are the numbers in the USA. While still growing slowly, nearly 78 per cent of the US population has an internet connection.

This means that if you don't have a website, you are missing out big time.

Now let me qualify that statement above: if you don't have a high-performing, quality website that is optimized for getting traffic, you are missing out.

If all you have is a website with contact information and a little bit about who you are and a place to sign up for a newsletter that you never really put out, then you are missing out nearly as much as those that don't have a website at all.

But this is only the beginning. Let's get into the rest of the data. While the internet market is still growing steadily, the mobile market is simply exploding.

The venture capital firm KPCB published a report called 'Internet Trends' and in it analyst Mary Meeker says that mobile devices now account for 45 per cent of all internet browsing.

The report also says, 'Mobile is huge, it's going to get tremendously larger, and will soon become... The Primary Way Most People Experience The Internet!'

It even goes so far as to say 'the Mobile Internet is becoming THE Internet.'

The mobile market in the USA is currently at 172 million people compared to 244 million regular internet users. That means that mobile use is up to 70 per cent of the size of the regular internet already.

Mobile internet traffic is currently 15 per cent of all internet traffic and is expected to continue growing one-and-a-half times per year.

With the explosion of smartphone and tablet ownership, how long do you think it will be before there are more mobile users than desktop users?

Research firm IDC projects that there will be more tablets shipped in quarter 4 of 2013 than desktops and laptops and that on an annual basis, tablets will be winning the war by the end of 2015.

So it's only a matter of time before the majority of visitors coming to your website, Facebook page, or whatever presence you have will be via one mobile device or another.

What exactly this means for your business

This means that you need to start thinking about how best to cater to these visitors. We recently had a real estate client that said that 40 per cent of his traffic was mobile!

And it's now common for sites to experience nearly 20–35 per cent of their traffic coming from mobile platforms.

Some points to consider:

Data from Google shows that 79 per cent of US smartphone users (iPhone, Android, Blackberry, etc.) use their browser **daily**.

Also from Google, nearly a third of all UK page views are from mobiles and tablets.

And people are not just searching and reading with their mobiles and tablets ... they're buying with them.

According to ComScore research, Amazon (the internet's largest retailer) has had year-on-year growth of sales made via mobiles of 87 per cent and Apple is seeing a 75 per cent growth of sales made via smartphones and tablets.

If you sell a product or provide a service, you need to make sure that your website can be easily viewed on a smartphone and tablet.

How do you find out whether you're already getting mobile visitors? Check your analytics software (or speak to your geek and get them to find out).

Alright so, maybe you are getting a lot of mobile traffic.

Do you know what to do with it?

Of course, if your mobile visitors aren't staying as long, you might need a better website with 'responsive design'.

This is when your website design files contain special code that detects what size screen and operating system the visitor is using. If it's one that could match a mobile device, it automatically gives that device the 'mobile' optimized version of the site.

Besides that, you might be tempted to treat them as just any other visitor to your site.

Why this is a bad idea

While a few of these visitors are probably browsing from home on their iPad, many of these (particularly those on their phones) may be checking out your site from across the street! Or while they are out and about and looking to purchase. These users then have massive potential for you and your local business.

For my real estate client, this meant that many people were seeing his 'for sale' signs and they were searching that address while looking at his sign.

Creating ads for mobile users

Create offers just for these visitors and pages that only they can see perhaps.

Think about what these visitors want from you and your business. Maybe you are a dog grooming business and you have a lot of mobile visitors. These visitors might have their mangy pooch sitting next to them in the car looking for a good service.

At the top of your mobile page should be something like 'Come to our location today, check in with Foursquare (or Facebook) on your mobile and get 20 per cent off!'

How likely would those visitors be to go and do that? How many dog owners do you think will come just because of that little ad? They might sign up for a Foursquare account just to get the discount ...

Well you won't know if you don't offer the option. Have a brainstorming session with your staff, and think about what someone that is sitting across the street would need to take action and give you a chance.

Another necessity of the mobile market

As well as your website needing to be mobile ready and having specific mobile ads, you also need to be checking your reputation on places like yelp.com and other local sites like Google Places.

These are most (if not all) mobile users' places of choice when it comes to finding a lot of businesses within a specific area from which to choose. With the right amount of SEO and some good reviews, you will be at the top of the search in no time.

Some of the key points on these sites are the following.

1 Make sure that you define the area you serve well.
   Don't target everyone within 1,000 miles (at least in the beginning). Aim for everything within 20–30 miles of your place of business.

   You do this by working on your site first, putting a page on your site targeting each area or sub-area within that bubble.

Also in the footer of your site, add all the zip codes (or post codes) with city names of the areas that you cover.

2 Next, register with Google Local, Yelp, Yahoo Local and Bing Local and set your area of service to the same 20–30 mile radius.

3 Next, start getting good reviews.

How to do this? Well asking for them helps. The tip is here, right after giving great service, as customers are on their way out the door, train your personnel to say that if they appreciated your service you would appreciate a quick review on X (where you need reviews at that point) service.

If you did a good job, many may whip out their smartphone right there and give the review.

You can also ask for these reviews via your email and address list as needed.

Start expanding

As you get a solid grasp of your core area, start expanding 10 miles or so at a time. Each time you do this, you will find it easier and easier to find new business. All the work you have done before will be building behind you.

These local strategies above, combined with a big social push on Facebook/LinkedIn with YouTube and a blog are absolute gold for your business as those services are very mobile-orientated as well (so everything you are learning in this book builds on this).

Run mobile ads/contests

If mobile ends up being big for you and your business, consider running ads targeting mobile users only on Facebook, Google Adwords and more. These customers, compared to how much time they spend on their mobiles, are only **10 per cent served**.

This means that mobile ads have little to no competition. Compared to the other areas of advertisement, this is almost the only area of real opportunity.

For instance, in newspaper advertising, compared to how much time people on average spend in the medium, it is saturated with over ten times more ads then the time warrants.

> ## Note
> A note for you if you are running newspaper ads. Now is probably the time to drop them unless you know that they are bringing in more business than they are costing.

Taking this to the next level

Okay, so you now have some ideas to start engaging the mobile user but there is a whole other level of integration that takes place when you enter a mobile user's life.

First some more stats to chew on:

- Mobile units (smartphones/tablets) overtook desktop/notebook computers in total amounts of shipments in 2010.
- The installed base (i.e. how many of these devices are actually in use) of mobile units is predicted to beat desktop/notebooks **this year** and nearly double the desktop/laptop market by 2015.
- This means that in only two years there will be twice as many mobile devices to check your site out than there are computers.
- With the resurgence of mobile operating systems, Android and Apple are now shipping more operating systems per year than Windows.
- This doesn't mean they are going to overtake Windows in installed bases soon but what it does mean is that Windows has a long way to go to break into the mobile market (as they have tried and so far failed to do) and even buying up Nokia's smartphone division may be too little too late.

With this mobile marketplace, people are now taking everything mobile. Now I want to talk a bit about where we see this shift in culture today.

Knowledge is now mobile

A recent study showed that while people were unlikely to know certain well-known facts, 90 per cent of the people that didn't know those facts knew where to find the answer online quickly if they had too.

This is also happening in the mobile world. People increasingly don't know where your business or others really are. But they do know where to go to find that information.

Now, instead of having to know everything they can whip out their mobile phone and do a search for up-to-date information.

Do you remember the last time you looked at an Encyclopedia Britannica?

Nope, me neither. They don't make them anymore. They went the way of the dodo with the advent of Wikipedia and Google.

Photographs have gone mobile

Instagram, Facebook, Flickr and more all cater to a market that uploads photos on the go.

In fact, every smartphone produced now has a camera in it that can take high-quality photos just like digital cameras.

In fact, stand-alone digital cameras are becoming more of a professional product then a consumer product as shipments of all stand-alone cameras peaked four years ago and have yet to recover.

TIP

Super ninja tip
Create a contest with photos where people put in a tag and do something with your product. For instance, taking the example of a pet grooming service, it could be take the best photo you can of your freshly shaved pooch and get the most likes on Facebook and Instagram and your next shave is free!

Books are going mobile

Kindle e-books now outsell print books on Amazon nearly three to one. In the first quarter of 2012, e-books outsold hard cover books in dollar terms!

As nice as it is to snuggle up with a book, people find it just too much to cart around many hardcover books. It is much easier to buy a book online and download it on any device they happen to have handy.

Navigation is becoming mobile

Just as stand-alone digital cameras are dying so are stand-alone GPS systems. Waze (which is a program that crowdsources mobile devices such as Android and iPhone), recently added more users than there were individual GPS devices shipped.

This is not counting mobile technology or people using Google or Apple Maps as a whole but just one app that helps with directions.

Notebooks/cabinet files are going mobile

Not only are the obvious things going mobile but even note-taking via Evernote, Dropbox, and other services are making documents and notes you have made accessible by just a few taps of your finger.

Wonder if that invoice has been paid? Check your Dropbox …

Magazines/newspapers are mobile

Print is dying ever so slowly but pretty much everything is going online and by extension everything is also going mobile. Why wait monthly to find out the colours for this season if you can log on right now and find them out as you are putting on your make-up at the mirror?

Why wait till tomorrow morning to find out what is happening in the news today when you can find out instantly on Twitter from the very people making the news? Or via the online versions of the newspapers?

All brought to us by mobile technology.

What this really means

The reason I have gone to such great lengths is to show that everything that can go mobile is going mobile. So what does this mean for your business?

This means that you should go mobile as much as possible. Position yourself early or you will find yourself playing catch up.

As you hopefully see by now, this means much more than just having a mobile-enabled website.

Level 1 Mobile integration with your business

This means, using the example of the dog grooming service, that you might consider doing an on-demand service actually going to your clients' homes. To make it even easier, provide a subscription service for those that want it and set times when you will come to their house to shave their beloved pooch.

These are the things that the mobile generation desire. They want something that does what they want when they want it. They want something that does everything in one thing, that is, the iPhone.

For those businesses without a physical service, you can start meeting your customers and demonstrating your services and products while they are on the go. Using such methods as GotoWebinar or Google Hangouts, you can meet your customers online and give them a presentation, with you and them being located anywhere in the world.

So, how you can start doing something now can be summed up in one sentence: Find out how you can go to your customer where they are now – without them having to come to you.

Level 2 Mobile integration

This involves getting involved in your clients/customers lives on a very real level without having to 'do' anything.

This involves a few different working parts that automate your business to the point of absurdity almost.

For the physical service

For instance, with the dog grooming service, create an app, that:

1 Reminds the customer that it is time for a hair cut for their dog.
2 Gives them a place to choose which cut they want on their dog this time. It should also give an option to write in what they want if the pre-selected options you have don't quite fit.
3 Gives a way to order right from their phone (if they aren't subscribed already).

See how this integrates you into their lives? They never have to see it done; they could be off in Africa for all you know but you have the order, the payment and what to do without doing anything but having an app made.

For the service provider

Let's say you are an accountant. You could create a similar app that could:

1 Remind clients to send in their monthly figures.
2 Notify them of upcoming changes to laws.
3 Give them the ability to upgrade/downgrade their service level directly via the app.
4 Publish exclusive special reports or white papers to only those people with the app. Use titles like '3 Ways To Legally Keep An Extra £5,000 in Your Pocket At Year End'.

I mean who wouldn't want to download an app just to read that?
Once again, you integrate yourself into their lives so that it becomes seamless.
This is just the tip of the iceberg. Sit down and brainstorm this hard until you figure out how you can position your business for the mobile explosion before it is too late!

Summary

Mobile is here and it is exploding at an incredible rate that may make the internet explosion look like a firecracker in front of a nuclear bomb (OK a little over the top but give me a break, I thought it was cool).

You need to get on the band wagon right now otherwise you will be one of those that get left behind scratching their head wondering at other businesses' success.

Get moving, start looking around at all the things that are going mobile and align yourself and your business to cater to mobile users. They want things right now and on their terms. They want to push some buttons and forget about it. They don't mind paying a little more if they have to think a little bit less and get the job done.

Take these underlying themes and run with them. If you position yourself just right at this point you can ride this wave for many, many years ahead.

Let's consider ten questions again shall we?

SUNDAY MONDAY TUESDAY WEDNESDAY THURSDAY FRIDAY SATURDAY

Questions

1. Mobile technology is:
a) Essential ❏
b) Optional ❏
c) Boring ❏
d) Rude ❏

2. You should put off changing to meet the mobile wave for:
a) Months ❏
b) Years ❏
c) Days ❏
d) Minutes ❏

3. In the next 1–2 years:
a) Things will be about where they are now ❏
b) Mobile users will outnumber desktop users ❏
c) There will not be desktops anymore ❏

4. Amazon's purchases via a mobile device have increased:
a) 25 per cent ❏
b) 52 per cent ❏
c) 60 per cent ❏
d) 87 per cent ❏

5. You should treat mobile visitors like any other visitor to your site.
a) True ❏
b) False ❏

6. Mobile ads are only how many per cent served:
a) 5 per cent ❏
b) 10 per cent ❏
c) 30 per cent ❏
d) 50 per cent ❏

7. Foursquare and Facebook are both:
a) Social media ❏
b) Good for getting people to check in at your location ❏
c) Places that your business should be findable on ❏
d) All of the above ❏

8. 90 per cent of people didn't know basic information but those same people:
a) Had no idea where to find it either ❏
b) Knew where to find it online ❏
c) Guessed good and got close ❏

9. What has gone mobile in one way or other?
a) Navigation ❏
b) Notebooks ❏
c) Books ❏
d) Notes ❏
e) Knowledge ❏
f) All of the above ❏

10. What should you consider to get mobile clients?
a) Meetings with Gotowebinar ❏
b) Creating an app ❏
c) Being more 'on demand' ❏
d) Being more flexible and going to your customers ❏
e) All of the above ❏

FRIDAY

Email marketing – why you should do it no matter what

Ok so that title may seem pretty bold but it really isn't.

Email is often overlooked as an effective marketing medium because it just isn't as 'sexy' as tweeting or Facebooking, Instagramming, or whatever other social network updates you do, but the truth is email marketing is far and away the best way to reach consumers on a personal level.

If you call your customers, they hate you for bothering their day and if you write them a letter, while cool (and a great potential way to break through the 'noise'), it costs actual real money to send to large numbers of people.

If you're targeting potential clients to offer high-end services, I recommend using personal letters or even FedEx to really get their attention, but for the average value client or visitor, I recommend email every time.

Email

Some facts on email that could blow you away:

- Email marketing's return on investment (ROI) for 2011 was $40.56 for every $1 invested. The figure for 2012 was slightly worse at $39.40, when email accounted for $67.8 billion in sales.
- A 2012 survey of consumer channel habits and preferences found that 77 per cent preferred to receive permission-based promotions via email: 6 per cent preferred such messages via social media. A similar survey of UK consumers found 69 per cent with a preference for email as the channel for brand communications.
- The 2012 Marketing Channel and Engagement Benchmark Survey found that 63 per cent of respondents cited email as the channel offering the best ROI.
- A survey of online marketing managers at the end of 2011 found 89.2 per cent said that email is the same or more important to their overall marketing strategy when compared to two years ago.
- In April 2011, 79 per cent of search marketers said that email had grown in importance as a source of leads.
- 72 per cent of respondents to an E-consultancy survey in early 2011 described email's ROI as excellent or good. Only organic SEO scored better.

Email needs to be done right though.

If it's done incorrectly, it's worse than not doing it at all.

It really breaks down into two separate categories:

1 Make sure that your email is received
2 Next, make sure that your email is read *and* responded to.

Making sure that your emails are received

If you go to all the trouble to write emails, you had better make sure that they actually hit your prospects' and clients' inboxes.

While this isn't so much of an issue when emailing directly from you to them, when you want to send messages to multiple

respondents at the same time (for example, if you're sending out an email newsletter), then things get a little sticky.

Most internet service providers (ISPs) will limit the number of emails that you can send out per hour and per day, so you can't just repeatedly blind carbon copy the 5,000 people in your prospect email database and hit send in Microsoft Outlook.

Even if you manage to get the emails sent, if you keep doing it you run a very good risk of having your company's domain name (the one you use in the From: setting in your email software) added to email spam blacklists that ISPs use to block emails from reaching their customers.

You also run the risk of your ISP thinking that you're spamming and simply disconnecting your internet access.

To eliminate this possibility, you have two real choices.

Sign up with a dedicated email marketing service provider like Aweber.com, GetResponse.com, iContact.com, Mailchimp.com. They have arrangements with the major ISPs that enable you to increase the chances of your email getting to your prospects and clients.

You benefit from the trust that the ISPs have with these email marketing service providers that they monitor and will stop as much spam as possible from being sent in the first place.

With most email marketing service providers, every email you compose will be evaluated for trigger words and phrases that could unintentionally flag your email as spam, enabling you to rewrite them accordingly.

You will also be evaluated by the number of 'spam' reports your emails generate from users, which will see your deliverability numbers diminish and then, ultimately, your account will be shut down.

Roll your own email marketing solution.

There are a number of software programs out there that can be installed onto your website or separate server that will enable you to run your email marketing system.

Two excellent programs I can recommend are ARPReach and Interspire Email Marketer. Both of these are very high-quality offerings with lots of features and functions with excellent support and installation help.

In years gone by, you would have needed a very high-end server set up to be able to run an email marketing system using this type of software but now with the advent of third-party email sending services like SMTP.com, Amazon SES and SendGrid.com, you can get the best of both worlds.

Both ARPReach and Interspire Email Marketer are able to directly interface with these external email sending services so you have 100 per cent control over the data, services like Amazon SES handle the server-intensive tasks of actually sending the emails and you get to benefit from their similar arrangements with the main ISPs.

Which route you take, email marketing service provider or roll your own, is up to you. If you don't have technical people on staff or you're not technically minded, go with option 1, otherwise take a serious look at option 2.

How to minimize your undeliverable emails

One way is to make people confirm their subscription request (sometimes known as 'double' opt-in).

This is when a visitor submits their details and then is told to click a link in an email just sent to them to confirm that they want to receive your emails.

Confirmed opt-in email subscribers have much higher engagement rates and email open rates, not to mention deliverability.

However, there is a drawback. In my experience only around half of the people who are told to confirm their request will actually do so, so you *will* lose some subscribers, either because it's 'too much effort' to go back to check their email and click a link, or they just never receive that confirmation email.

You can't really do anything about it if they never receive the confirmation email but another way to stop them from *not bothering* to confirm is to make sure that they have something significant to *gain* by subscribing.

My advice is don't bother with trying to get people to subscribe to receive an email newsletter.

Newsletters are seen as 'boring' and unless yours has amazing information in it every issue, people just won't subscribe. Better to just send them great, actionable information on a regular basis.

Send reports, white papers with cutting edge info and links to YouTube videos you've uploaded with ground-breaking news that directly affects them.

Think about how best to stand out from others in your industry and make sure that whichever method your 'ethical bribe' content is released by, it's not just vague, general information but very *specific* to the kind of client or customer you're looking for.

TIP

Marketing tip

One tactic that some business owners are beginning to use is to write a quality report on their area of expertise and publish it in Kindle format on Amazon.

There are lots of videos showing you how to do it on YouTube and it can be done totally free (if you're doing it yourself) or you can hire someone from a freelancer website like oDesk.com or eLance.com who will format and set up the book on Amazon.

Why go to the trouble to do this?

Because then you can give the book/report away for free with a 'As sold on Amazon for $x.xx' statement on the page.

Do you see the power of this? First, it uses Amazon's credibility to build yours (you're a published author now) and at the same time gives the information an actual $$ value, regardless of the value the reader will get from the information within.

Whether you actually sell books on Amazon is irrelevant. Your visitors now have a good reason to jump through one extra hoop to get your book.

Getting your emails read

So now you know your preferred clients got your free 'ethical bribe' with $x.xx – now what?

Ask them to buy something!

Nooooooooo! Don't do it! (reaches out hand in slow motion)

Resist this temptation like the plague – this just isn't cool.

You don't propose to someone on the first date. You need to build up a relationship with the other person before you go down on bended knee, so to speak.

Give even more quality, useful and helpful information for free to your potential clients. With the email marketing service providers and the two software programs I mentioned before, you can pre-load entire sequences of emails to be sent automatically over a period of time, each and every time someone signs up.

Don't worry about giving away too much information. There's no such thing. If you're a service provider, you may be concerned that all your subscribers will simply take all the information you give them and do it all themselves.

They won't. Not everyone has the time or the inclination to figure stuff out on their own, especially if you're marketing to business owners. Of course some will, but most won't and those are the people who will seriously think about contacting you for help. (Kind of like me and this book, some might say.)

Fill in the holes and give further advice regarding the issue or good idea that you solved in the first give-away product.

TIP

If you're still not 100 per cent sure about giving away lots of free information, don't go into deep specifics – just tell them 'what' has to be done to get the benefits but not exactly 'how' to do it.

Make them look forward to seeing your brand name in the inbox. This 'trains' them to always open your emails. Now when you send them that offer for a discount on your product or consultation, they will hear you out.

Don't stop sending good information. Make it a habit to continually be sending out good information to your email list.

One publication I follow sends out a 'reading list' of things across the web that he has found during the past week that are good reading for his particular audience.

It is a mixture of stuff from his own hired bloggers and other websites and is usually pretty informative.

Other ideas for fun and profit

Depending on the type of business you have and who your customers and clients are, you might be able to build up engagement and rapport with your subscribers by:

- Running competitions like 'xx of the Month' or 'Funniest xx' and share the results on your Facebook page.
- Posting links to interesting videos you find on YouTube created by others (who aren't in direct competition with you) and explain exactly why people should watch them.
- Finding other people offering similar services that don't directly compete with you who might want to reach your subscribers and try to cross-promote one another to each other's lists by offering useful information.

If I had to start over

If Google blasted my websites into oblivion, Facebook banned my fanpages, and my dog abandoned me the only thing I would really need are my trusty email lists.

Those lists are all I really need to generate revenue because they are people who are interested in the things I am interested in.

I know what they probably want and from that list I could make money to keep me going until I got a new website and a new fanpage.

Your prospect and client email lists are an essential business asset that you should be building, because they really are the foundation of digital marketing and where all the money is at.

Summary

The difficult part is finding the perfect mix of information and sales pitch. Try and lean as far you can to information first and test out various levels of 'sales' to make sure that you don't overdo it with your particular market. Each one has their own tolerance level for sales but can never get enough good information from an expert for free.

Don't worry if you slightly overdo it; just go back into educational mode and people will quickly remember why they joined your list in the first place.

Remember: good information, good information, good information, sell.

Wash, rinse, and repeat.

The thing about lists is if you treat them right they can be responsive for years and years.

If you treat them or neglect they will quickly unsubscribe and spam folder your emails (simply because they might forget signing up to get your emails).

And here are some questions to make sure it sinks in:

SUNDAY

MONDAY

TUESDAY

WEDNESDAY

THURSDAY

FRIDAY

SATURDAY

Questions

1. Email is often overlooked because:
a) It isn't 'sexy' ❏
b) It's boring ❏
c) People think it bothers people ❏
d) All of the above ❏

2. ____ per cent of people prefer email though (according to some studies):
a) 73 ❏
b) 35 ❏
c) 56 ❏
d) 96 ❏

3. You need to be sure with email that:
a) Your email is received ❏
b) Your email is read ❏
c) Your email is responded to ❏
d) All of the above ❏

4. It is recommended that you get the following if you don't have a tech team:
a) Aweber or equivalent ❏
b) ARPReach ❏
c) Interspire ❏
d) All of the above ❏

5. The best opt-in is:
a) Double opt-in ❏
b) Single opt-in ❏
c) Personal preference ❏
d) Secret opt-in ❏

6. Giving something away of value to get people to opt-in is:
a) A bad idea ❏
b) A waste of time ❏
c) Smart ❏
d) Sort of cool but not that cool ❏

7. After people opt-in:
a) Send them an offer ❏
b) Send them 500 offers one after the other till they buy ❏
c) Never send them any offers, just wait till they ask to buy from you ❏
d) Send a bunch of more free amazing content, then an offer, followed by more free content and another offer ❏

8. Free information (including telling your clients exactly how to do what you do):
a) Is a good idea ❏
b) Makes them less likely to pay you ❏
c) Makes you appear to be the expert ❏
d) A and C are correct ❏

9. If they don't buy the first time you email them:
a) Take them off your list ❏
b) Keep sending good info ❏
c) Curse them ❏
d) Send them a virus ❏

10. If I had to start over, I would need:
a) SEO ❏
b) Social media pages ❏
c) My email lists ❏
d) A website ❏

SATURDAY

Other marketing tricks and tips in the modern world

Up till now, we have talked about the basic foundations of digital marketing today. First, build a killer sales website, then get traffic to your website with SEO, social media marketing and then pay-per-click paid traffic.

After that, we talked about the two other ways to reach your customers – leveraging the huge growth in mobile usage and, possibly one of the most overlooked ways, email marketing.

Today, I want to talk about several other methods you can use to get traffic that, when combined, can really generate a ton of traffic.

Online press releases

Many people will tell you that these are old-fashioned and to leave them alone if you want to reach people.

This is not the case.

People still want news, they want to know the latest gizmos, gadgets, and trends.

As such, press releases might not be for every business, though you are probably different as you are reading this book.

If you follow my advice from yesterday, you may create an app. If you have created an app, why not create a press release 'Want to pamper your pooch by phone? NY dog grooming service says "There's an app for that!"

This is news that is worth reading and worth spreading around. Other people will read this even if they aren't dog owners, just to see the latest trend. You could even end up in the *New York Times* if you play your cards right (see instructions below).

Press release best practices

1. Always be newsworthy

When you start talking about online press releases, there are many SEO benefits as well. Do your best to ignore these and just produce real news.

Feature other related businesses to highlight a trend or do something a bit crazy to get publicity or maybe broadcast how you are giving back to your community with free dog bath Saturdays or something.

Be unique but, most of all, actually *be* interesting news. This will come in handy later.

2. Keep it short and also have video and pictures

This is the best way to make your press release stand out and get attention.

- Make it about 300 words but then include great images (worth a thousand words) and a short video less than three minutes long (worth a million words).
- Newsreaders and more importantly reporters have incredibly short attention spans and you will lose them really fast unless you write short and to the point and include attractive photos. If they are really interested, they can then watch your video.
- Even if they don't use the video and pictures should they cover your story, it can be worth it just to get their attention.
- If you need help writing and promoting your press release, you can Google search terms like 'press release services' or

go to a freelancer site like oDesk.com or eLance.com and hire someone to write and promote it for you.

- If you fancy taking a crack at it yourself, there are tons of books on Amazon on press releases and getting free publicity and you can search on Google for terms like 'free press releases templates' and 'how to develop a press release hook'.

3. Release at 10 a.m. on Tuesday

Why then? Because it is most likely to be noticed at that time due to the lack of other news going on. This time is usually when 'the lag' hits in the week, despite the fact that news is a 24-hour business.

4. After the release do a little leg work

Sometimes, even if you make your press release interesting and do the above, it still won't get noticed because of all the 'noise'.

Have a list of the top publications that your customers/ clients will most likely read, for example, for our company in New York, their clients probably read the *New York Times* and a few other local papers.

Literally call these places, right after the release (remember it is during a lull, you should get through).

Go directly after the most relevant reporter (for instance, if you're an independent financial advisor, the reporter will be the one that writes about personal money matters).

Call attention to your press release and tell them what it's about. If they want to look at it right away, then be sure to have the release already featured on your home page. So all you have to do is give them your cute URL for them to see it immediately.

Be sure and get their email during this exchange as well (for the future).

Whether they end up publishing or not, you now at least have an email address to send to the next time you have a release.

In conclusion to press releases

Doing the above can bring massive traffic and credit in the eyes of the world and Google.

Only do it when your website is in good shape with lots of content and you have all the other foundation pieces in place that we have mentioned in previous days.

Otherwise your well-earned traffic will be wasted.

Yahoo Answers and Quora

These are both places people go for answers to questions and a great place to establish yourself as an expert.

Quora in particular is becoming more and more the mobile and social media answer of choice and the best place for you to really customize your image because they allow a lot to be placed in your profile page, though Yahoo Answers is still often at the top of Google for many searches.

Both are still valuable and worth looking into for your business.

How to use them

Give insightful and detailed answers only to questions in your specific niche. Use your equally insightful and relevant blog post as a source on Yahoo Answers (be sure and write out the link with http:// included) or as a 'for more info click here' link on Quora.

That is about it.

Pros and cons

If you look at the most popular posts on Quora, you will see that they use mostly images, and long detailed answers to get to the top. But getting yourself to the top is well worth it.

When a post gets popular on Quora, there is an email that goes out to everyone that has expressed interest in that subject and you will be amazed at the traffic you can achieve to your site.

Yahoo is not so drastic or immediately evident but requires less of an investment in time (the questions are usually very much to a specific solution, not so broad and deep as Quora questions).

Sample Quora question:

What is love?

Sample Yahoo Answers question:

How do I get rid of this zit on my big toe?

This is a bit of a generalization because there are bigger questions on Yahoo Answers too!

In my tests and former projects, however, I have seen ten visitors or so a month per question answered.

This may not seem like much but if you answer 100 questions (not hard to do) this means around 1,000 visitors a month.

Plus there are even ways to outsource Yahoo Answers as there are established and professional 'answerers' out there willing to plug you into their answers. (This is not something you would want to do on Quora however.)

In conclusion

These two sources of traffic aren't good for every business. Be sure and check them out if you decide to use them. Give incredible content and answers and you will have fantastic results, both with real quality traffic *and* your SEO efforts as the links do count despite the fact they are 'no follow' (at least according to my tests).

Guest blogging

This is all the rage right now – both rightly and wrongly so. The idea is essentially finding an authority blog in your niche and then writing a high-quality post for that site to get a link and bring traffic back to your site.

This is good when starting out and even better with G+ authorship now available but they aren't everything to traffic and SEO that others make them out to be.

So you do get credit for the post both in Google's eyes with G+ and the readers there. But it still also gets credited to the blog you posted on and the click through rates on blog posts tend to stink. (They are not that much better than Yahoo Answers.)

They require a lot of time and effort both to get the post and to create the perfect content. And wouldn't it be better if you spent that time on your site and business? Just a thought …

The best way to make this work I would think is to outsource it. Have 5–10 fantastic pieces of content created with pictures and everything. Then have someone look around for a blog willing to post them.

That should be all you need for credibility in this arena with Google and should let you know whether they are worth it (use Google Analytics to track which authority blogs are sending you traffic and which aren't – concentrate on the ones that are).

HARO (help a reporter out) http://helpareporter.com

This is a great site that allows you to sign up both to be a source for a reporter's story and also a place to find people to write stories about on your site.

How does this work?

Well first you go and sign up. Once you reach a certain level of traffic (lower than a million on the Alexa.com scale at the time of writing), then you can be a reporter.

There are no restrictions for being a source.

What happens is that there will constantly come into your mailbox 20–30 reporters that ask for a certain type of people to be 'sources' for their stories. This is one of the many places that all the experts end up with lines on online stories.

Becoming a source is good if you are dedicated to it. Essentially you will have to constantly check the emails as they come in and apply to each one that you are suited for. It is usually good to offer your services on one unique subject as well, as otherwise you will not stand out to the reporter (they get hundreds of responses).

They usually then ask you a set of questions and you get a mention in their article with a byline.

Cool.

But the most power comes from actually being the reporter. I once had it set up with one of my projects that I would put out a call for a certain group of people and suddenly I had my pick from all sorts of well-qualified people to appear on my blog.

The way I set it up was to give them a full interview either over the phone or just via email.

This got me absolutely tons of exposure, not just for my website (where I started ranking for these peoples' names); but also exposure on their websites, as many of them promoted my website as a place where they were featured.

I ended up interviewing one of the biggest names in this field with this technique on the first try, and ended up getting a free pass (retail value $1,000) to a conference in my area.

So, once you get the traffic, start running interviews on HARO – you'll be amazed where it can get you.

Rolling with the Twitter giants

Twitter is a great place to get people following your brand but it is an even better place to find big names in your industry with which to interact and get them to literally promote you to their followers.

So how this works is, first of all, research your niche. For our usual example of the dog groomers in New York, they might look for dog trainers in New York, or reporters that write about pets and/or the home, or even celebrities that have dogs in New York.

Find them and start following them (don't start spamming them or anything – nothing will get you removed faster).

Get to know them and the things they tweet. During this time, be sharing your own musings and good content as well connecting with your followers (i.e. keep it real).

Then when you see something pretty cool or related to you, retweet it, or write a comment to it. Do this consistently and do it well and you will see them eventually check you out and, if you have good content, they will follow you.

Now as the relationship deepens you can @ sign them on things that you know they will find cool (remember, you have been watching them, you little stalker you).

Eventually you will be landing deals, getting retweets and getting featured in newspapers that you would never believe possible and wouldn't be possible any other day except today.

You may end up like the guy who asked Kate Upton to the prom and actually got a call, only cooler because you will make money off of it, not just high fives from all your friends.

Viral marketing

Ah, the holy grail of digital marketing, how we all long for our material to go 'viral'. For those unsure of what this means, it means that your stuff gets shared, then shared, then shared some more and next thing you know you are on *Good Morning America* yucking it up with Oprah.

While there is really no way to know if something is going to go viral or not, there are some things to do to give it your best shot. (Below I will use the example of videos, but the things talked about can be any medium, from a blog post to an image you produce that gets shared a million times on Facebook.)

Looking at the list of most viral YouTube videos of 2012, you can note that most of them were well-produced videos.

In other words, they were professionally produced pieces that appealed to the video maker's followers immediately.

This is a good place to start. Don't try to make something that goes viral by being stupid and putting up junk funny videos unrelated to your niche.

Make sure that your videos will appeal to your kind of people first. This way, if it does go viral your kind of people will like it and want to visit your website.

Also, even if it doesn't go viral the views/traction you do get will only build your brand more for the next try.

Next, you will note that many of the videos that went viral were funny. Particularly the number 1 most viewed video of all time.

Humour really gets people to take notice and everyone likes to share something that makes them laugh.

As long as it isn't racist, sexist, or anything with else with '-ist' at the end of it, let your sense of humour be on full display. Don't be that boring guy that takes everything so serious.

If humour is not your style, then hire someone who can be more light-hearted if you want any chance at viral success.

TIP

Go to your local comedy club and watch a few of the acts. See who you like and see whether you can have a quick chat with them afterwards. You'll be surprised how cheaply you can hire someone to help you come up with a funny approach.

Next, make quality content to the right length. This can't be overemphasized. Make them as long as they need to be; there is no magic cut-off point for length. One of the top ten videos from 2012 was over 30 minutes long! So this could mean making your viral blog post 2,000 words long.

If you follow the above steps, it will not guarantee that you will go 'viral' but it will guarantee that you resonate with your fans/followers and so on – which is never a bad thing. Eventually, no matter how you slice it, you will get traffic from it.

So at the point that you finally go viral, it might just be icing on the cake and not so much a necessity for fame and fortune.

Summary

These were my super tips for building your brand and name. Use them for good and not for evil!

There will always be more and possibly better websites that may replace those that I have mentioned today. If you find them, jump in with both feet when you get a chance.

'There is no such thing as bad press' rings true even here. The more you get your name and brand out there the better.

For those new sites you may find and for the sites I mentioned above, remember it is always good to give a lot of good content and link to your website when it calls for it and always in context. You never know where some of these rabbit holes will lead, but I can say with certainty if you don't go out and promote yourself on these places and others, no one else will do it for you.

At least to start you are your own best promotion machine. Depending on how well you do it, it will pay off for years at a time, because most of what you do on the sites

SUNDAY

MONDAY

TUESDAY

WEDNESDAY

THURSDAY

FRIDAY

SATURDAY

I mentioned will stick forever, continuing to drive traffic till the web collapses due to nuclear apocalypse (or whatever).

Here are some questions to help them stick a little bit better:

Questions

SUNDAY
MONDAY
TUESDAY
WEDNESDAY
THURSDAY
FRIDAY
SATURDAY

1. Today is all about:
a) Getting traffic from Google ❑
b) Getting traffic from outside Google ❑

2. Press releases are:
a) Still effective today ❑
b) Old fashioned ❑
c) Useless ❑
d) Nice but too expensive ❑

3. Yahoo Answers and Quora are exactly the same.
a) True ❑
b) False ❑

4. Yahoo Answers is more for specific questions about how to do something.
a) True ❑
b) False ❑

5. Quora usually requires more thought and care in how you answer than Yahoo Answers.
a) True ❑
b) False ❑

6. Guest blogging:
a) Is the best traffic source imaginable ❑
b) Is not all it is cracked up ❑
c) Should be outsourced ❑
d) Both b and c ❑

7. HARO stands for:
a) Hi are you rolling OK? ❑
b) Hold already ramping one ❑
c) Help a reporter out ❑
d) Handy Arnold rounded over ❑

8. When you start following someone on Twitter you really want to:
a) Be cool and get to know them first ❑
b) Spam them with all you got ❑
c) Get to know them, then spam them ❑
d) Spam them and all their followers ❑

9. One type of person to follow is:
a) Experts in your niche ❑
b) Reporters in your niche ❑
c) Celebrities that like your niche ❑
d) All of the above ❑

10. To turn a piece of content viral:
a) Put it into a viral machine ❑
b) Turn around three times and wiggle your nose ❑
c) Be humorous and resonate with your existing audience ❑
d) Spam people with junk videos of your kids playing on the playground ❑

CONCLUSION

Surviving in tough times

The times are tough, economies all over the world are uncertain; you yourself might find yourself in difficult times with not a lot of money or time to spend on your website to reach your goal of freedom with your new-found digital marketing skills.

To that end I've included the following tips to help you to still be able to implement what you have found in this book to its fullest.

1. Have a plan

Have a goal of where you want to be in one week, one month, three months and one year and stick to it as best you can. Think about how many visitors you will need a day, and the conversion rate to customers that you would need to be able to quit your day job (if that is the case with you), be able to break even with your business, be able to take that vacation or buy that car with the proceeds or even just make this month's sales targets. Dream and aim big.

2. Do a little work each day

First and foremost, set time aside each day to do something on your business. You may find yourself stressed and short on time but don't let this make you put off creating your super sales website. The turtle really does win the race if you keep it up and don't compromise your quality. For your site this could mean putting together just one amazing, incredible multimedia experience only once a month. This is still better than nothing at all.

3. Make maximum use of all the social networks

This means Facebook, Twitter, Youtube, et al. You probably use these networks in some way already. So use them for your potential business as well. Commit to one quick post at the beginning of the day and the end. Post images (do a search on Flickr for a fun/interesting/slightly controversial image) or make one yourself with any of the free image editing software out there. Also, grab related videos from YouTube or sit down in front of your computer and use a free screen capture program or webcam to create one yourself (http://camstudio.org), just make it fun and informative. Then post it to your Facebook page and tweet it.

When you are on social networks, be social and real.

Most of all, make full use of social media by being fun and likable. At the same time, always use a call to action (ask them to like or share your content). Being real and asking for action all the time will naturally make people want to share, both you and your content. To save time in this area, use Hootsuite, a free program that will let you post, tweet and more from one website.

4. Web design on the cheap

If you are doing things low cost, use WordPress.org and a good-looking free theme from there for your website to begin with. While this may seem like it would hurt your chances, it is not hard to tweak the website enough to make it look totally new and unique to you and even if it isn't, the reason people are visiting is for your useful and fun content, not your million-dollar design. As long as you have a website that doesn't distract your customers because of its awful design, you should be fine (at least to start). Pay for a killer design later once you start making money ...

5. Use plug-ins

If you are using WordPress use as many good rated plug-ins as you can find to make your life as easy as possible. Do not go overboard here and try to automate everything (because, at the end of the day, manual is best). Search on Google for lists of the best to use.

6. Niche down as much as possible

Do not try and sell everything in the world in an effort to make money. Doing this, you may ultimately make nothing. Clearly define your 'niche' and make it as specific as possible, with enough searches every month to keep it profitable. When you do this, you will find it easier and easier to rank for your keywords as well.

7. Link-build naturally and as cheaply as possible

Focus on the free methods given on Saturday, because these give both links but more importantly traffic. Spend as little time as you can doing this. If you have the ability, outsource some of these to someone on oDesk.com to do it. This is well worth the investment.

8. Little to no cash = avoid PPC

If you find yourself short on cash, do not use PPC or any other paid traffic as doing this wrongly can lead to you getting into debt to Google and others and that can only hurt your efforts in the long run. Use this only after you are making some money from your sites. The sole reason to use PPC at this stage would be to spend some money to test the conversion rates of your landing page(s) to make sure that they convert. Be sure to turn it off quickly once you hit your limit though.

9. Avoid all the get-rich-quick stuff out there, as well as timewasters

As you get more and more involved online, avoid get-rich-quick schemes but avoid most of all wasting time. There are hundreds of ideas out there just on how to use YouTube videos or Facebook or Pinterest, and on and on it goes. Find what works for you to create good material and keep going with that till you break through. Don't keep getting distracted with the latest trend to the detriment of creating fun posts and content. The latest shiny plug-in is cool and all but don't become a plug-in collector without also being a content generating machine.

Answers to questions

Sunday: 1b; 2b; 3c; 4c; 5d; 6a; 7e; 8a; 9a; 10b

Monday: 1b; 2a; 3c; 4d; 5c; 6b; 7c; 8a; 9d; 10a

Tuesday: 1c; 2d; 3b; 4g; 5b; 6a; 7d; 8c; 9b; 10a

Wednesday: 1c; 2f; 3c; 4a; 5b; 6d; 7e; 8c; 9a; 10a

Thursday: 1a; 2d; 3b; 4d; 5b; 6b; 7d; 8b; 9f; 10e

Friday: 1d; 2a; 3d; 4a; 5c; 6c 7d; 8d; 9b; 10c

Saturday: 1b; 2a; 3b; 4a; 5a; 6d; 7c; 8a; 9d; 10c

Notes

ALSO AVAILABLE IN THE 'IN A WEEK' SERIES

BODY LANGUAGE FOR MANAGEMENT • BOOKKEEPING AND ACCOUNTING • CUSTOMER CARE • DEALING WITH DIFFICULT PEOPLE • EMOTIONAL INTELLIGENCE • FINANCE FOR NON-FINANCIAL MANAGERS • INTRODUCING MANAGEMENT • MANAGING YOUR BOSS • MARKET RESEARCH • NEURO-LINGUISTIC PROGRAMMING • OUTSTANDING CREATIVITY • PLANNING YOUR CAREER • SPEED READING • SUCCEEDING AT INTERVIEWS • SUCCESSFUL APPRAISALS • SUCCESSFUL ASSERTIVENESS • SUCCESSFUL BUSINESS PLANS • SUCCESSFUL CHANGE MANAGEMENT • SUCCESSFUL COACHING • SUCCESSFUL COPYWRITING • SUCCESSFUL CVS • SUCCESSFUL INTERVIEWING

SUCCES COPYWR

Sunday: Sunday – work out what you want to say
Monday: put yourself in your readers' shoes
Tuesday: learn the art of letter writing. Wednesday: understand advertising
Thursday: become a popular press commentator
Friday: discover why most promotional print says too
Saturday: explore some of words

LEARN IN A WEEK
WHAT THE LEAD
LEARN IN A LIFE

ROBERT ASHTON
LEADING EXPERT AN

SUCCESSFUL NEGOTIATING

Teach Yourself

Sunday: Learn how to set up the best "environment" for a negotiation Monday: Know how to research and plan your objectives Tuesday:Consider variations in the venue a meeting Wednesday: Explore the opening me the meeting Thursday: the best ways of moving negotiation forward Frida negotiation to a satisfactory how you can continue to grow skills

LEARN IN A WEEK
WHAT THE LEADING EXPERTS
LEARN IN A LIFETIME

PETER FLEMING
LEADING EXPERT AND TRAINER

IN A WEEK

For information about other titles in the series, please visit
www.inaweek.co.uk

ALSO AVAILABLE IN THE 'IN A WEEK' SERIES

SUCCESSFUL JOB APPLICATIONS ● SUCCESSFUL JOB HUNTING ● SUCCESSFUL KEY ACCOUNT MANAGEMENT ● SUCCESSFUL LEADERSHIP ● SUCCESSFUL MARKETING ● SUCCESSFUL MARKETING PLANS ● SUCCESSFUL MEETINGS ● SUCCESSFUL MEMORY TECHNIQUES ● SUCCESSFUL MENTORING ● SUCCESSFUL NEGOTIATING ● SUCCESSFUL NETWORKING ● SUCCESSFUL PEOPLE SKILLS ● SUCCESSFUL PRESENTING ● SUCCESSFUL PROJECT MANAGEMENT ● SUCCESSFUL PSYCHOMETRIC TESTING ● SUCCESSFUL PUBLIC RELATIONS ● SUCCESSFUL RECRUITMENT ● SUCCESSFUL SELLING ● SUCCESSFUL STRATEGY ● SUCCESSFUL TIME MANAGEMENT ● TACKLING INTERVIEW QUESTIONS

For information about other titles in the series, please visit www.inaweek.co.uk

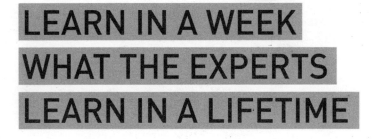

For information about other titles
in the series, please visit
www.inaweek.co.uk